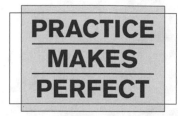

PRACTICE
MAKES
PERFECT

The Spanish
Subjunctive
Up Close

PRACTICE
MAKES
PERFECT

The Spanish Subjunctive *Up Close*

SECOND EDITION

Eric Vogt, PhD

Mc Graw Hill Education

New York Chicago San Francisco Athens London Madrid
Mexico City Milan New Delhi Singapore Sydney Toronto

1 2 3 4 5 6 7 8 9   LCR   22 21 20 19 18 17

ISBN   978-1-260-01074-9
MHID   1-260-01074-0

eISBN   978-1-260-01075-6
eMHID   1-260-01075-9

Interior design by Village Typographers, Inc.

McGraw-Hill Education books are available at special quantity discounts to use as premiums and sale promotions, or for use in copyright training programs. To contact a representative, please visit the Contact Us pages at www.mhprofessional.com

Contents

Preface

Are you tired of a lot of song and dance about what the subjunctive is and how to use it correctly? Well, it's time to get to know the subjunctive up close. Although many reference grammars and textbooks cover the topic, too many treat it hastily or in a haphazard fashion. Have your textbooks or—God forbid!—your teachers confused you with list after list of verb phrases and conjunctions, trying to get you to understand what the subjunctive *means* to native speakers of Spanish? Do your eyelids droop even in the daytime, or your teeth clench at the sound of the word *subjunctive*? If so, this is the book for you.

As often happens when one is confused by a subject, you may need to unlearn before you can relearn. If this is your first exposure to the subject, then this book will save you from the abyss of confusion resulting from the numerous ill-conceived, incomplete, or diluted ways in which the subjunctive has often been treated.

Intermediate to advanced learners can profit from this book and begin to conquer the feared subjunctive in three or four weekends of systematic study. *Practice Makes Perfect: The Spanish Subjunctive Up Close* has been designed for people who have been or are being exposed to the subjunctive in any sort of language program. It is ideal as a stand-alone text for independent study or review or as a complementary text to any existing textbook, either for when the subjunctive is first introduced or in a grammar review or conversation class. The only tenses you need to know well to use this book to maximum advantage are the present indicative and the preterite.

Whoever the user of this book might be, one thing is certain: I'll tell it like it is about the Spanish subjunctive and tell you what you need to do to learn it and use it correctly. Here, you'll find all the facts, nothing withheld or spread out over weeks of chapters but all presented boldly and progressively, with exercises and answer keys that do more than just give the right answers. You'll find many answers explained, in English, from the psychological perspective of a native speaker of Spanish. So take the time to follow my advice as you study. It will be as if I were standing next to you while you do your homework. I promise to demystify what has been too often overcomplicated or incorrectly presented in many books I've seen in twenty-five years of teaching. I promise I won't mince my words. And if you promise yourself to study it carefully and thoughtfully, putting the concepts to work in your oral and written use of Spanish, your communication skills in this beautiful language will improve a great deal. Next thing you know, you'll be fluent.

First of all, it is important to accept something many books don't openly declare: the subjunctive doesn't *mean* anything!

So, just what *is* the subjunctive, then? In a nutshell, it is *a set of verb forms required in clauses of certain types*. Trust me. That's all it is, and that succinct definition is what I am going to unpack in this book. The subjunctive is *hardwired* into the *architecture* of the language, if you'll forgive my mixed metaphors. In translation, the difference between a Spanish speaker using an indicative or a subjunctive form often disappears; that is, it conveys no meaning in and of itself, but that *doesn't* mean it isn't important. It's essential. Sure, honest attempts in all sorts of textbooks will offer English translations in which you'll see the word *may* or *might* before an English verb to try to show what the subjunctive is *doing* in the original Spanish. Since *may* and *might*, as counterparts of the subjunctive, only work sometimes, they seldom are enough to emotionally or intellectually *convince* language learners, or earn their trust. After all, if the function of the subjunctive was solely to convey uncertainty, why not just say **tal vez** (*perhaps*) before an indicative and forget about the subjunctive? But then, if that were enough to explain the essence of the subjunctive, how would one explain that **tal vez** is an expression often, but not always, followed by the subjunctive?

Clearly, something must be done to clear all this up! By the way, if you don't know what the terms *clause* or *indicative* mean, you may need to look them up before you continue. A standard dictionary—or, better yet, an English grammar reference—will quickly bring you up to speed with all the terminology you need.

Being noticeably foreign can have negative or positive connotations. You may wonder why you can't just get by without the subjunctive, and the answer is, of course, that you *could*, but you would forever be a marginal participant in the Spanish-speaking world. A person who speaks or writes broken English will get by too, but he or she remains cut off from much of the richness of American cultural life. If you consider the impression you'll make on native speakers of Spanish and don't care about the consequences of speaking *subjunctivelessly*, then don't buy this book, or, if you have already, I hope you kept your receipt.

A brief anecdote may be helpful to convince you of the need to take this subject seriously. I once knew a woman who had been inexplicably placed in a responsible position to negotiate with high-level administrators in Mexico. Prior to embarking on what would prove to be a cultural embarrassment to the organization she represented, because she had convinced the right people that she spoke Spanish, she confided to me in an ironically boastful tone that she spoke Spanish *fluently* but quickly added, ". . . oh, except for that subjunctive in those compound tenses and 'if' clauses." The exasperating thing was that she could identify her exact problem but had not taken the time to solve it. Since one use of the subjunctive is to express hypothetical situations, her lack of ability to manage the subjunctive made it impossible for her to negotiate in Spanish and interpreters had to be called in at important moments.

The subjunctive opens the door to the knowledge and understanding of feelings, emotions, and proverbs, and, in true and meaningful ways, to the cultures of the Spanish-speaking world. To be subjunctiveless is to remain forever culturally disadvantaged, having only a superficial understanding of cross-cultural communications.

So, imagine the possibilities! With a command of the subjunctive, you will go beyond the rudimentary business associated with travel, hotel stays, and buying a meal or a souvenir. By manipulating the subjunctive with confidence, you'll be able to progress beyond the grunt-and-point method of casual tourists. You'll be able to wheel and deal, make plans in love and business, with all their *what-ifs* and *how-abouts*, conditions imagined, proposed, or anticipated.

Just as you may have experienced, or may yet be experiencing with the preterite and the imperfect, there will be other milestones or hurdles in your continued quest for mastery of Spanish, but none will be possible until *this* Everest is scaled. You stand at the foothills. With *Practice Makes Perfect: The Spanish Subjunctive Up Close*, I'll be your sherpa.

I think you're a believer now. Ready? Here we go.

Acknowledgments

To all my students of Spanish, known and unknown, present and future, real or virtual, with special thanks to all those who have in various ways contributed to the fine-tuning of this presentation on the Spanish subjunctive. Many thanks to my daughter Alexandra, who, while in high school, brought this book to the attention of her classmates. And a special acknowledgment to my friend and former colleague Lylje Klein for her keen eye and sharp mind as she read successive iterations of the drafts of the first edition of this work.

When to use the subjunctive and how to form its four tenses

The study of the subjunctive involves understanding four things. The first is what the subjunctive is. Second, it is essential to know how to form the four tenses of the mood known as the subjunctive. Third, by examining the specific clause types in which the subjunctive is often required, one will know when—and when not—to use it. Last of all, if the subjunctive must be used, one has to know how to select the correct one of this mood's four tenses.

Definition

The best overarching and practical definition of the subjunctive is that it is *a set of verb forms required in clauses of certain types.* It is important to absorb this as a mental framework on which to place the corresponding sets of rules for deciding whether the subjunctive is needed or not. The rules that work in one set of circumstances will not apply in another.

Many students of Spanish have been led to believe that the subjunctive is all about doubt and uncertainty on the part of the speaker, but this is only *one* aspect of *one* clause type. To depend on such a definition does more harm than good to one's learning. If uncertainty or doubt were the whole explanation of the subjunctive and were predictive of when it needs to be used, then it would be correct to say **Juan sea médico**, which is not a grammatically correct sentence, no matter what the speaker believes, suspects, wishes, or doubts. What is *is*, regardless of one's attitudes about reality, right? This is why the need to use or not use the subjunctive is not determined by what is thought, or even what one knows or believes is true, but rather by the types of clauses involved.

Clauses

It is essential to be able to identify the clause type, apply the corresponding rule, and then, if the subjunctive is needed, choose the correct one of the four tenses of the subjunctive mood.

Because it may be necessary to review what a clause is, that will be one of the first items addressed before we can deal more specifically with the types of clauses in which the subjunctive may be required. A clause is a group of words with a grammatical subject, understood or expressed, and a conjugated verb. That sounds like what a sentence is, doesn't it? In fact, that is correct. Some clauses are stand-alone sentences:

> *The boy is tall.*
> *The computers work.*
> *There are four birds on the roof.*

The clauses that concern learners of the Spanish subjunctive are *not* the stand-alone or *independent* types but the *dependent* ones. Dependent clauses are said to be *subordinated* to the main idea of an introductory clause. They tell the listener *what* is asserted by the speaker.

The independent clauses above can become subordinated, or dependent ones, too:

> *Jane hopes that the boy is tall.*
> *We prefer that the computers work.*
> *We know that there are four birds on the roof.*

In these three longer sentences, the assertions *Jane hopes*, *We prefer*, and *We know* are used to introduce, or set up, the clauses that previously were stand-alone sentences. Everything in these sentences from the word *that* to the end makes up what is known as a *subordinated* or *subordinate clause*. The introductory clauses, simple as they are, *can* stand alone as grammatical sentences. Granted, it isn't clear *what* is hoped, preferred, or known. The answer to that question is what the dependent or subordinate clause supplies. Precisely *what* it is that Jane hopes, *what* we prefer, and *what* we know is found in the subordinated clauses. Stated as they now are in our second set of sentences, these subordinated clauses cannot stand alone: *that the boy is tall*, *that the computers work*, and *that there are four birds on the roof*—stated just like that—simply are not grammatically correct sentences.

The next important thing to notice is that they are introduced by the word *that*, a conjunction, or joining word. Think of it as mortar between bricks, if you like building metaphors, or couplings connecting railroad cars if you need another analogy.

English-speaking learners of Spanish need to keep in mind that the word *that* can be omitted in English without harming the message or being ungrammatical. In Spanish, if an assertion is placed in a subordinated position, the corresponding conjunction, or word linking the two parts of the sentence, the connective word—**que**—must be used. Although it is true that in business correspondence it often is omitted, it is best to learn to use it before learning when it can be omitted in such specialized modes of communication.

The four types of clauses in which the subjunctive may be necessary are:

◆ Subordinated noun clauses
◆ Subordinated adjective clauses
◆ Adverbial clauses
◆ Hypothetical or contrary-to-fact statements

Once the forms of the subjunctive are mastered, the decision-making process is reduced to identifying *the type of clause* involved and then applying the corresponding set of rules to determine whether the subjunctive is needed. Last of all, the rules about sequence of tense will determine which of the four subjunctive forms to use—if, in fact, the subjunctive is needed.

The four tenses of the subjunctive

Your first goal is to know how to form the four tenses of the subjunctive.

Let's start with some basic definitions. The *tense* of a verb refers to the *time* in which the action it expresses occurs. Infinitives have no tense. Their possibilities might be seen as being limitless, as opposed to the conjugated forms, which are *finite*, precisely because they have been fixed in a time frame and assigned person and number—that is, a subject (or doer) of the action. The endings of conjugated verbs are what show person and number. This correspondence between subject and verb ending is called *agreement*.

It may come as a pleasant surprise to learn that the grammatical term *mood* refers to the *attitude* of the speaker regarding the action, as in the *imperative*, *potential*, *infinitive*, or *participial* moods. In English, moods are expressed by *modal* verbs that introduce infinitives—for example, by auxiliary or helping verbs such as *can*, *could*, *should*, *would*, *must*, *might*, *may*, *will*, and *shall*. In Spanish, these ideas are expressed by verbs such as **poder**, **deber**, and others, as well as by the use of the *subjunctive* and *conditional* moods, and therefore the verbs are fully inflected, with a set of six endings, one for each person and number. So, logically, the four tenses of the subjunctive mood appear in all persons and numbers of any and all verbs.

Unfortunately, there is no set of one-to-one rules to show how Spanish handles the English modal verbs. This is partly because there is not a neat, one-to-one correspondence between the number of modals in English and the number of solutions these may have in Spanish. There are no dependable sets of rules for which verb forms, or even which Spanish helping verbs, to use when going from English to Spanish. Therefore, it is important, first, to be aware of this fact and, second, to internalize the logic of the Spanish verb system by becoming attuned to its own logic.

In modern Spanish, there are four *tenses* of the subjunctive. This book will not deal with the future subjunctive or the future perfect subjunctive, which nowadays are mainly relegated to proverbial usage and legal documents. For those interested in them, their forms are not difficult to learn.

The *present indicative* and the *preterite* are the two tenses that must be thoroughly known before tackling the subjunctive forms. All the irregularities found in all four tenses of the subjunctive will be easily recognized and probably remembered once these two tenses are committed to memory.

The present subjunctive

To form the *present subjunctive* use the **yo** form of the present indicative and, for -**ar** verbs, change the -**o** to an -**e** and, for -**er** and -**ir** verbs, change the -**o** to an -**a** and then proceed to conjugate the resulting form, adding the personal endings as in the indicative. Notice that this procedure can make it appear that **hablar**, for instance, has become an -**er** verb, while **comer** and **vivir** have become -**ar** verbs. *That is not the case*, of course, so the lesson here is to reference all forms, recognizable by their stem (e.g., **habl**-), to their proper infinitive ending:

hable	habl**emos**	coma	com**amos**	viva	viv**amos**
habl**es**	habl**éis**	comas	com**áis**	vivas	viv**áis**
hable	habl**en**	coma	com**an**	viva	vivan

For verbs that are irregular in the present indicative: if the irregularity is a *consonant change* that shows up in the **yo** form of the present indicative, this change is found in *all three persons*, *singular and plural*, in the present subjunctive:

ten**g**a	ten**g**amos	conozca	conozc**amos**
tengas	ten**g**áis	conozcas	conozcáis
ten**g**a	ten**g**an	conozca	conozc**an**

Likewise, if the irregularity is a *single-vowel-to-single-vowel* one, then this irregularity is found in *all persons and numbers*:

sirv**a**	sirv**amos**	pid**a**	pid**amos**
sirv**as**	sirv**áis**	pid**as**	pid**áis**
sirv**a**	sirv**an**	pid**a**	pid**an**

If *both* are present in the **yo** form, then, once again, *both show up all the way through* the present subjunctive:

dig**a**	dig**amos**
dig**as**	dig**áis**
dig**a**	dig**an**

For verbs that have a single vowel to diphthong (double vowel) change in the present indicative, this change continues to follow the shoe or boot pattern:

piens**e**	pens**emos**	pued**a**	pod**amos**
piens**es**	pens**éis**	pued**as**	pod**áis**
piens**e**	piens**en**	pued**a**	pued**an**

Finally, there are a handful of verbs whose present subjunctive forms are best learned by memorizing. The present subjunctive forms of **dormir** and **morir** are formed as in the shoe-pattern verbs above, but their **nosotros** forms are **durmamos** and **muramos**. Even these can be organized into rhyming pairs: **ir** and **haber**, **vaya** and **haya**, respectively; and **ser** and **ver**, **sea** and **vea**, respectively; and, of course, **saber**, whose present subjunctive forms begin with **sepa**, which rhymes with the somewhat rare verb **caber** (*to fit*), whose present subjunctive forms begin with **quepa**!

The imperfect subjunctive

To form the *imperfect subjunctive* begin with the *third-person plural of the preterite* (the **ellos**, **ellas**, **ustedes** form). For *all* verbs, simply remove **-on** and replace it with **-a** and begin conjugating again, using it as a new **yo** form, and adding the personal endings.

You may have learned or seen that there is an alternative form of the imperfect subjunctive that ends in **-se** (e.g., **tuviese** instead of **tuviera**). It is not used in this book, being somewhat more used in literary settings than in speaking, in most regions. In any event, the rules for using this alternative form are, stylistic matters aside, the same.

Generally, the irregular verbs in the preterite cause more problems than the irregular verbs in the present, because so many verbs have a new stem in the preterite that can't be derived by any logical rules. However, once the new stems are known, the formation of the imperfect subjunctive is uniformly achieved in the following way: from **tuvieron-** > **tuvier-**, one begins by adding **-a** and proceeding like this:

tuvier**a**	tuvié**ramos**
tuvier**as**	tuvié**rais**
tuvier**a**	tuvier**an**

It should come as truly good news that this rule works perfectly for all three families of verbs (-**ar**, -**er**, and -**ir**), both regular and irregular, so that the imperfect subjunctive forms of **hablar**, **comer**, and **vivir** are all derived from the third-person plural of the preterite, in just the same way as the imperfect subjunctive of **tener**.

The present perfect subjunctive

The *present perfect subjunctive* corresponds to its indicative form just as the present indicative relates to the present subjunctive. There are two chief obstacles for mastering this form. The first is to learn the six forms of the present subjunctive of the helping verb **haber**, which is quite irregular; that is, you cannot predict its form based on the indicative. As shown on page 5, it rhymes with the present subjunctive of **ir** (**vaya**...):

INDICATIVE		SUBJUNCTIVE	
he	hemos	haya	hayamos
has	habéis	hayas	hayáis
ha	han	haya	hayan

The second obstacle is knowing how to form the past participle. For -**ar** verbs whose past participle is regular, remove the -**ar** and change it to -**ado** (**hablar** > **hablado**). For -**er** and -**ir** verbs whose past participle is regular, remove the -**er** or -**ir** and change them to -**ido** (**comer** > **comido**; **vivir** > **vivido**). This second obstacle contains another small challenge. There are only a baker's dozen of irregular past participles, if one does not count compounds built with them, such as **resolver**, based on **solver**:

abrir	abierto	morir	muerto
cubrir	cubierto	poner	puesto
decir	dicho	romper	roto
escribir	escrito	solver	suelto
hacer	hecho	ver	visto
imprimir	impreso	volver	vuelto

To form this tense of the subjunctive, use the present subjunctive of **haber** and combine it with the past participles. It is easy to see that the present perfect subjunctive form **hayas comido** corresponds to the indicative form **has comido**. Both translate into English as *you have eaten*, but the subjunctive one must be used in certain types of clauses.

The pluperfect subjunctive

As one might suspect, this subjunctive form corresponds to the pluperfect indicative. The same observations regarding irregular past participles used to form the present perfect indicative and subjunctive are in force in the formation of this tense of the subjunctive. The imperfect subjunctive of the helping verb **haber** combined with the participles form this tense. Just as the present perfect subjunctive corresponds to the present perfect indicative, this subjunctive form corresponds to the pluperfect indicative. Thus **había comido** and **hubiera comido** both translate as *had eaten*, but the subjunctive one is used in certain types of clauses. Observe the following contrasting examples:

Pluperfect indicative

Cuando **llegamos a casa** vimos que el perro **había salido** del garaje.	*When we **got home**, we saw that the dog **had gotten out** of the garage.*
Juan **supo** que su novia no le **había sido** fiel.	*John **found out** that his girlfriend **had cheated** on him.*

Pluperfect subjunctive

Dudábamos que el perro **hubiera salido** del garaje.	*We **doubted** that the dog **had gotten out** of the garage.*
Juan **no pudo creer** que su novia le **hubiera sido** infiel.	*John **couldn't believe** that his girlfriend **had cheated** on him.*

The indicative examples rarely cause English speakers any problem. What learners need to remember is that both **había** and **hubiera** translate into English as *had*. The only difference is in the need for the subjunctive.

It is important to remember that in the subjunctive examples it does not matter whether the speaker, in the moment of uttering these sentences, knows whether or not the dog had gotten out of the garage or whether it turned out or not that John's girlfriend had been faithful. In the case of the dog, the main clause is introduced by a statement of doubt, in the past. The dog may or may not have gotten out prior to the speaker's arrival. In the second case, the main clause contains a statement of disbelief. By the time John arrived at his moment of incredulity, his girlfriend either had or had not cheated on him. Grammatically, whether she did or did not, the subjunctive is required.

For each of the following verbs, give the present subjunctive form for the
person and number indicated.

EXAMPLE   tú/poder ___puedas___

1. ella/pensar ___piense___

2. vosotros/creer ___creáis___

3. yo/decir ___diga___

4. nosotros/tener ___Tengamos___

5. él/ver ___vea___

6. Ud./ser ___sea___

7. yo/haber ___haga___

8. tú/ir ___vayas___

9. ellos/dar ___dénin___

10. yo/dormir ___duerma___

11. yo/conocer ___conozca___

12. tú/saber ___sepas___

13. ella/conducir ___conduzca___

14. Uds./hacer ___hagan___

15. vosotros/escribir ___escribáis___

16. yo/sacar ___saque___

17. él/pagar ___pague___

18. Ud./empezar ___empiece___

19. nosotros/concluir ___concluyamos___

20. ellas/estar ___estén___

For each of the following verbs, give the imperfect subjunctive *form for the person and number indicated.*

EXAMPLE   tú/poder ___pudieras___

1. tú/estar ___estuvieras___
2. ellas/saber ___supieran___
3. nosotros/poner ___pusiéramos___
4. Ud./poder ___pudiera___
5. ellos/morir ___muriera___
6. yo/tener ___tuviera___
7. Uds./ver ___vieran___
8. ella/dar ___diera___
9. él/ir ___fuera___
10. ellas/haber ___hubieran___
11. yo/ver ___viera___
12. Ud./ser ___fuera___
13. tú/pagar ___pagaras___
14. vosotros/andar ___anduvierais___
15. yo/hacer ___hiciera___
16. Ud./trabajar ___Trabajara___
17. él/conducir ___condujera___
18. ellas/leer ___leyeran___
19. vosotros/hablar ___hablara___
20. tú/comer ___comieras___

For each of the following verbs, give the present perfect subjunctive form for the person and number indicated. Remember that a dozen common verbs have irregular past participles!

EXAMPLE   tú/poder   _hayas podido_

1. ella/cubrir   haya cubrido

2. yo/escribir   haya escrito

3. vosotros/hablar   hayáis hablado

4. tú/ver   hayas visto

5. él/morir   haya morido

6. yo/dormir   haya dormido

7. vosotros/comer   hayáis comido

8. ella/abrir   haya abrido

9. nosotros/hacer   hayamos hecho

10. ellas/comer   hayan comido

11. yo/saber   haya sido

12. yo/decir   haya dicho

13. tú/ir   hayas ido

14. yo/vivir   haya vivido

15. él/cubrir   haya cubrido

16. vosotros/venir   hayáis venido

17. ellos/poner   hayan puesto

18. tú/conocer   hayas conocido

19. yo/romper   haya roto

20. él/conducir   haya condacido

For each of the following verbs, give the pluperfect subjunctive *form for the person and number indicated.*

EXAMPLE   tú/poder   *hubieras podido*

1. yo/cantar   hubiera cantado

2. ella/abrir   hubiera abierto

3. él/ver   habiera visto

4. nosotros/destruir   hubieramos destruido

5. ellas/obtener   habieran obtenido

6. Ud./castigar   hubiera castigado

7. tú/verificar   hubieras verificado

8. Uds./sistematizar   habieran sistematizado

9. vosotros/descubrir   hubieráis descubrido

10. yo/conocer   hubiera conocido

11. ellos/hacer   hubieran hecho

12. yo/mentir   hubiera mentido

13. vosotros/conducir   habieráis conducido

14. tú/servir   hubieras servido

15. él/fabricar   hubiera fabricado

16. nosotros/pedir   hubieramos pedido

17. ella/sobornar   hubiera sobornado

18. Ud./romper   hubiera roto

19. yo/decir   hubiera dicho

20. tú/escribir   hubieras escrito

Sequence of tenses and the subjunctive

·2·

Now that you have learned the forms of the subjunctive, we need to take a close look at the four tenses of the subjunctive as they relate to what is known as sequence of tenses. Understanding which tenses can or must be used in subordinated clauses, introduced by main clauses in which the various indicative tenses are used, will enable you to use the proper subjunctive form, if it is required according to the rules for a given clause type. Even though this is the last step in the decision-making process, you now need to comprehend the *temporal logic* of the four forms you have just learned to form. You'll learn that the choice of subjunctive has nothing new to say about grammar per se, at least in terms of when to use the subjunctive or indicative, and everything to do with temporal logic. Once this logic is clear, you will have the confidence to tackle the exercises following the explanations of the clause types, in which any of the forms of the subjunctive could be needed.

Whether or not this is your first exposure to the subject, it is good to clarify what is meant by sequence of tenses. So, we'll begin with an illustration of the rules for sequence of tenses by comparing four sentences.

Many grammar books point out that the subjunctive, considered collectively or per se, is not a tense but rather a *mood*, and that it is in the four forms of the subjunctive where one finds that there are four tenses of this mood. Likewise, most textbooks mention that the rules for using the subjunctive are the same, regardless of tense, and they almost always dedicate some time and space to the concept of sequence.

So, *which* subjunctive is the *right* one once you know you need to use it? As you'll see in the examples that follow, the choice depends on the time of action of the main verb—this is what is meant by *temporal logic*.

People can express *emotions* about things that are, that were, that have been, that had been, or that may yet be. Thus, verbs that express emotion are ideal for illustrating the principle of sequence of tenses and its internal logic. The examples that follow all use the subjunctive in subordinated noun clauses. You will learn all about this clause type later, but for the sake of examples designed to illustrate the temporal logic of the sequence of tenses, the main clause contains a verb of emotion, introducing a subordinated clause with its own subject and verb—which is why, according to the rules of the game of Spanish grammar, the verb in that clause must be subjunctive. Through this handful of examples you will be enabled to observe the internal temporal logic behind the native speaker's choice of subjunctive. It is important to know how to apply the principle of sequence of tenses in order to use the subjunctive properly in three of the clause types we shall explore later when we study subordinated noun clauses, adjective clauses, and adverbial expressions.

To internalize this logic, it is highly advisable to *memorize* the examples that follow, along with their translations, so you have a model on the tip of your tongue. In the exercises, or in your oral practice of the language elsewhere, *imitate* their usage of the subjunctive. Use them as models for sentences of your own. They need to be in your head so you can learn to express your own thoughts; after all, we only truly know what we can remember and use. The good news is that these are the only patterns there are for management of the sequence of tenses. In a nutshell, don't overanalyze! Memorize them and imitate them! In the following introductory examples, the word **ojalá** (from an Arabic expression meaning "May Allah grant") stands for the entire independent clause. In the translations of the examples below, I have used "I pray to God that" because it is more natural to English speakers' ears.

The *present subjunctive* is used when the action of the verb is in either the present or the future. Thus, in the following example, the party is either in progress or it is being planned. It is likely that John will yet come to the party, if it is in progress, or will come to it, if it is just being planned.

<table>
<tr><td>Ojalá que Juan venga a la fiesta.</td><td>I pray to God that John comes to the party.</td></tr>
</table>

If the party is actually going on, then the *present perfect subjunctive* is used to express an action that has taken place and whose influence is still in effect. Thus, in the following example, the party is actually going on, the speaker has not seen John yet, but is quite hopeful that John is there.

<table>
<tr><td>Ojalá que Juan haya venido a la fiesta.</td><td>I pray to God that John has come to the party.</td></tr>
</table>

In the following example, the speaker uses the *imperfect subjunctive* to express a strong doubt about John's attendance at the party. There are two possible scenarios. If the party is in the planning stage, the speaker is highly doubtful that John will accept. If the party is in progress, the speaker views John's arrival as so highly unlikely, or contrary to the current reality, that he or she uses the imperfect subjunctive. In this latter scenario, the use of the imperfect subjunctive is temporally equal to the present perfect subjunctive in the preceding example, and, in fact, the speaker could have used that form to express the same doubt. What has happened is that the speaker's attitude about John's arrival goes counter to his or her observation of facts or expectations. Because the imperfect subjunctive, as you will see later, is used to express counterfactual propositions, this was the form that first came to the native speaker's mind.

Ojalá que Juan **viniera** a la fiesta.	*I wish to God John **were coming** to the party.*

The *pluperfect subjunctive* is used for an action that is viewed as prior to some other action in the past. Thus, in the following example, the party is not only over but John's arrival is viewed as something that (logically) would have had to have occurred before the party ended. In other words, and quite simply—John never showed up.

Ojalá que Juan **hubiera venido** a la fiesta.	*I wish to God that John **had come** to the party.*

The temporal logic needed to manage sequence of tenses can be seen in more recognizable independent clauses by using verbs of disbelief or doubt in different tenses in the independent clause to introduce the subordinate clause. In the following examples, therefore, **ojalá** has simply been expanded into a more readily recognized independent clause—with an obvious subject and conjugated verb. For some learners, this construction is more helpful than the previous set of examples using **ojalá**, even though the lesson is exactly the same.

These comparisons show the usage of the four subjunctive tenses and how they are related temporally to the seven simple, indicative tenses and the two conditional ones (simple and compound). You might want to review these tenses as you examine these examples.

The following examples serve as reminders that not all types of verbs in an independent clause will necessitate the use of the subjunctive in the subordinate clause. This will be taken up in more detail in the chapter on subordinated noun clauses. For now, pay attention to the choice of subjunctive in the examples and how each depends, temporally, on the tense of the verb in the independent clause. It is the verb in the main clause that sets the temporal tone, so to speak.

Indicative: Creo que ella **viene.**
Subjunctive: No creo que ella **venga.**

*I believe she **is coming.***
*I don't believe she **is coming** (or **will come**).*

Indicative: Creo que ella **vendrá.**
Subjunctive: No creo que ella **venga.**

*I believe she **will come.***
*I don't believe she **will come** (or **is coming**).*

In the preceding two examples, the present subjunctive has both present *and* future force, as seen previously when using **ojalá** as our entire independent or main clause.

A comparison of the Spanish and English in the following example shows why it is better to view the subjunctive as a form that has no meaning—it's just a verb form that has to be used in certain situations, but one that has four tenses that must be used according to the temporal logic of the verb system. Also note that the *present perfect indicative* (*has come* = **ha venido**) has its corresponding subjunctive form (*has come* = **haya venido**) to be used when the subjunctive is necessary.

> **Indicative:** Creo que ella **ha venido**.   *I believe she **has come**.*
> **Subjunctive:** No creo que ella **haya venido**.   *I don't believe she **has come**.*

Note that in the following example the *future perfect* in Spanish indicates probability in the present—one of the peculiar uses of the future tenses in Spanish. A somewhat longer English translation would insert the word *probably* or some other word to express wonder or supposition.

> **Indicative:** Creo que ella **habrá venido**.   *I believe she **has come**.*
> **Subjunctive:** No creo que ella **haya venido**.   *I don't believe she **has come**.*

The following example (the last in which the present tense is used in the independent clause) shows how a belief or disbelief can be expressed in the present about a past event. The Spanish use of the imperfect subjunctive (**viniera**) in this example contrasts very slightly with the previous example in which the present perfect subjunctive (**haya venido**) was used. The choice depends on the remoteness of the event, as was explained in the first set of examples using **ojalá**. The same reasoning is used in English when deciding between simple past (*came*) and present perfect (*has come*). The only additional factor in Spanish is that each of these English words has both indicative and subjunctive solutions, depending on the clauses in which they appear.

> **Indicative:** Creo que ella **vino**.   *I believe she **came**.*
> **Subjunctive:** No creo que ella **viniera**.   *I don't believe she **came** (or **has come**).*

In the following example, the indicative sentence is a good example of the contrast between *preterite* and *imperfect*. The preterite is used to indicate a moment in the past when the speaker's belief about something occurred. The action expressed by the imperfect indicative could express her arrival as being either in progress with respect to the moment of speaking or yet future, as is the case with the English translation of this example. The subjunctive example shows what happens when the main verb of belief changes to one of disbelief.

> **Indicative:** Creí que ella **venía**.   *I believed she **was coming**.*
> **Subjunctive:** No creí que ella **viniera**.   *I didn't believe she **would come**.*

What is especially noteworthy is not that the imperfect subjunctive must be used, but that when the imperfect subjunctive is introduced by a past tense verb in the independent clause, the action expressed by the imperfect subjunctive can refer only to an action yet to occur—it becomes a sort of future-of-the-past tense. When introduced by a present tense verb, as seen above, the imperfect subjunctive can refer only to an action in the past (whether or not it really occurred is irrelevant from a grammatical point of view).

The only difference between the following and preceding examples is the use of the *conditional* (**vendría**) instead of the *imperfect indicative* (**venía**). Just as the *future* tense was used earlier to indicate probability in the present, one peculiar use of the conditional in Spanish is to indicate probability in the past. When changing an expression of belief in the past to an expression of disbelief in the past, the grammatical consequence for the subordinate clause remains the same—the imperfect subjunctive must be used.

> **Indicative:** Creí que ella **vendría**.   *I believed she **would come**.*
> **Subjunctive:** No creí que ella **viniera**.   *I didn't believe she **would come**.*

In the following example, the *imperfect indicative* is used instead of the *preterite* for the verb in the independent clause. This choice has *no* impact on the subjunctive in the example, where the belief shifts to disbelief. The lesson here is that when the verb in the independent clause is in any past tense, the present and present perfect subjunctives simply are not admissible choices in Spanish because they locate the action in a time frame that is impossible from the temporal perspective of the main verb. Consider how illogical it is to command someone to have already done something and the problems of sequence will be immediately obvious.

However, as previous examples have shown, when *present* tense verbs are used in the independent clause, the verb in the subordinate or dependent clause can be in any tense, depending on the meaning of the verb in the main clause. As was just observed, although it would be illogical to demand that something have happened already, it is perfectly possible to wish in the here and now that something *has happened*, *happened*, or *had happened* (prior to something else, please note!), depending on context.

> **Indicative:** Creía que ella **vino**.   *I believed she **came**.*
> **Subjunctive:** No creía que ella **viniera**.   *I didn't believe she **would come**.*

The last two examples that follow are like two previous pairs of examples (**Creo que ella venía/No creo que ella viniera** and **Creo que ella vendría/No creo que ella viniera**). The difference is that in these last two examples the action is shifted further into the past by the use of **haber** + past participle. Also, just as the present perfect indicative (**ha venido**) has a corresponding subjunctive form, the present perfect subjunctive (**haya venido**), the pluperfect indicative (**había venido**) has its corresponding subjunctive form, the pluperfect subjunctive (**hubiera venido**).

Indicative: Creía que ella **había venido**.
*I believed she **had come**.*
Subjunctive: No creía que ella **hubiera venido**.
*I didn't believe she **had come**.*

Indicative: Creía que ella **habría venido**.
*I believed she **had come**.*
Subjunctive: No creía que ella **hubiera venido**.
*I didn't believe she **had come**.*

Remember that the present subjunctive, the present perfect subjunctive, as well as the conditional and conditional perfect, must not be used with **si**, meaning *if*. This may seem as if it places a straitjacket on your mind, but the things you mean to say are all easily and properly said by following the rules. This does not mean you will never hear them used or never see them in print, or that the use of the **-ra** form of the imperfect subjunctive as an equivalent of the pluperfect indicative is not sometimes found (it is a vestige of classical usage, common in the Caribbean basin, not an error). But, aside from such regional oddities, remember that many native speakers of English make blunders in their own language. As a learner, it is wise to follow the standard until you are aware of the variants. After all, what kind of speaker of Spanish do you want to be and what kind of impression do you want to make?

Finally, do not be confused by the use of the conditional or imperfect subjunctive forms of the verbs **querer**, **deber**, and **poder** when they are used as auxiliary or helping verbs, which is what they are whenever they are followed directly by an infinitive. This aspect of the use of these three verbs has nothing to do with sequence of tense but needs to be pointed out in this context so that you can resist the temptation to try to find a reason for the use of these two forms. These three helping verbs can be used in the simple present indicative, the conditional, or the imperfect subjunctive, as shown below. When the present indicative is used, it likely will not cause any difficulty. But the other two, the conditional and imperfect subjunctive, can cause some learners to search through all the reasons for the use of the subjunctive—in vain, because in these limited circumstances, the choice of tense and mood does *not* change meaning (i.e., the time of the action or its likeliness). They only reflect degrees of politeness. Grammatically and morphologically, they are trifles, but socially and culturally, they can be a big deal. Examine the following three examples:

¿Puedes darme la guía telefónica?
***Can** you give me the telephone book?*
¿Podrías darme la guía telefónica?
***Could** you give me the telephone book?*
¿Pudieras darme la guía telefónica?
***Would you kindly** give me the telephone book?*

In all three sentences, the meaning or message is the same. The only difference derived from the choice of present, conditional, or imperfect subjunctive in the auxiliary verb **poder** is that the degree of politeness increases as you go down the list.

Knowing how **poder** works should make it relatively easy to intuit what impact the same choices have on **querer** and **deber**, even while recognizing that adequate translations into English often are elusive and may seem overpolite, pleading, or even obsequious (which they assuredly are not in Spanish, unless, of course, the tone is).

¿Quieres acompañarme al cine?	***Do you want*** *to go with me to the movies?*
¿Querrías acompañarme al cine?	***Would you like*** *to go with me to the movies?*
¿Quisieras acompañarme al cine?	***Would you, please,*** *like to go with me to the movies?*
Debes estudiar más si quieres sacar buenas notas.	***You should*** *study more if you want to get good grades.*
Deberías estudiar más si quieres sacar buenas notas.	***You ought*** *to study more if you want to get good grades.*
Debieras estudiar más si quieres sacar buenas notas.	***You really ought*** *to study more if you want to get good grades.*

Be sure to learn these three verbs well in the *present indicative, conditional,* and *imperfect subjunctive.* Their potential impact on social and cultural relations cannot be overstated and no number of cross-cultural communications classes or sensitivity training seminars can make up for not being able to use them correctly.

Do the following exercises if you had no major problems with the exercises on the forms of the subjunctive at the end of the preceding chapter. Although all clause types will be seen in all the following exercise sets, your task is greatly reduced by the assurance that the subjunctive is needed in all cases—which means you can focus on the problem of sequence of tenses and not on applying the proper set of rules to determine whether or not the subjunctive is needed. That will come later. Before continuing to the next chapter, check the answer key so you can remedy any remaining problems.

First identify the tense of the verb in the independent or main clause. It sets the temporal frame of reference. Then, according to what you have learned about sequence of tenses, fill in the blanks with the correct subjunctive form of the verb in parentheses.

1. Espero que mi amigo _tenga_ la paciencia necesaria para hacer el proyecto hoy. (tener)

2. Deseaba que tú _vieras_ la película con nosotros ayer. (ver)

3. Es importante que los estudiantes _vayan_ a clase todos los días. (ir)

4. Era urgente que ellos _leyeran_ el artículo antes de ir a clase. (leer)

5. ¿Quieres que yo _pague_ la cuenta en efectivo? (pagar)

6. Leímos la lección antes de que ellos nos _hablaran_ sobre el tema. (hablar)

7. Dudaban que él _pudiera traducir_ el libro antes de 2000. (traducir)

8. Mis amigos no creen que tú _puedas escribir_ tantos poemas. (escribir)

9. Necesito una novia que siempre _diga_ la verdad. (decir)

10. No querían que nosotros _escucháramos_ la canción antes de la fiesta. (escuchar)

11. Creen que es fantástico que yo _trabajara_ para mi padre. (trabajar)

12. No les gustó nada que yo _tuviera que renunciar_ a mi trabajo. (renunciar)

Match the following independent clauses on the left with their correct dependent clauses on the right, according to the rules for sequence of tenses. Although examples of many types of clauses that require the subjunctive are found, the lesson here is strictly confined to sequence of tenses decisions. There are other clues to help you match the sentences.

1. _c_ Deseamos...
2. _g_ Se alegró...
3. _h_ Mi amigo duda...
4. _f_ Buscábamos un gato...
5. _b_ Juan insistió...
6. _i_ Necesitas un carro...
7. _j_ Yo quería...
8. _d_ Su novia esperaba...
9. _e_ Quería una casa...
10. _a_ Espero...

a. ... que mi cumpleaños se celebre con un pastel.
b. ... que tú nos compres unas cervezas.
c. ... que Ud. vaya a venir a vernos esta tarde.
d. ... que él le comprara flores.
e. ... que tuviera una vista del mar.
f. ... que no peleara con el perro.
g. ... de que yo viniera a la fiesta.
h. ... en que ellas no lo acompañaran al cine.
i. ... que use menos gasolina.
j. ... que mis padres me dieran una bicicleta cuando yo era niño.

Multiple choice. Write the letter of the dependent clause that completes the sentence correctly according to the rules for sequence of tenses.

1. Los mecánicos esperan que _el jefe les pague mas por su trabajo_
   a. el jefe les pagara más por su trabajo
   b. hiciera buen tiempo
   c. el jefe les pague más por su trabajo
   d. tuvieran más tiempo libre

2. Los mecánicos esperaban que _____.
   a. el jefe les pagara más por su trabajo
   b. haga buen tiempo
   c. el jefe les pague más por su trabajo
   d. tengan más tiempo libre

3. Juana esperaba encontrar un novio que _____.
   a. le compre flores el día de su santo
   b. le llamara todos los días
   c. sepa bailar bien
   d. cante canciones románticas

4. Ahora, mi familia y yo buscamos un hotel que _____.
   a. no costara tanto
   b. sea económico
   c. estuviera cerca de la playa
   d. tuviera aire acondicionado

5. Tú me recomiendas que yo _____.
   a. me quedara en casa este fin de semana
   b. no comiera tanto
   c. duerma más de noche
   d. comprara un nuevo abrigo

6. Los políticos recomendaban que _____.
   a. todos paguen más impuestos
   b. los pobres trabajen sin descanso
   c. la clase media tuviera que pagar más impuestos
   d. los pobres dejen de trabajar

7. Mis amigos vinieron antes de que yo _____.
   a. pueda vestirme
   b. tuviera tiempo para cenar
   c. vea el noticiero
   d. regrese del trabajo

8. Voy al cine tan pronto como _____.
   a. tú vengas a buscarme en el coche
   b. tú vinieras a buscarme en el coche
   c. tú y tus amigos tuvieran tiempo para ver una película
   d. yo pudiera ponerme los zapatos

9. Sus padres le van a dar un coche a María con tal de que ella _____.
   a. consiguiera un trabajo estable
   b. encuentre trabajo
   c. se graduara de la universidad
   d. no se casara con Juan

10. Yo voy a Europa de vacaciones a menos que _____.
    a. no tuviera suficientes días acumulados
    b. haga mal tiempo en París
    c. hiciera mal tiempo en París
    d. tuviera que trabajar durante esa semana

Subordinated noun clauses

As you have read a few times thus far, there are four types of clauses in which the subjunctive may be required. Each type has its own unique set of rules to make this determination according to the type of clause involved. Because subordinated noun clauses are only one of the four types of clauses, how do you identify a clause as a subordinated *noun* clause in order to apply the proper rule to determine whether you need the subjunctive or not? After all, *all* clauses are composed of a noun and a conjugated verb. So how do you go about distinguishing a subordinated clause as a *noun* clause? The answer has to do with its relationship to the main clause that introduces it. A subordinated noun clause acts like a large direct object that answers the question of *what*, answering that question posed by the verb at the end of the main clause.

Yo deseo **que el maestro explique el subjuntivo**.	*I want the teacher **to explain** the subjunctive.*

Notice that in English, the construction is quite different from Spanish. English uses what is known as an *accusative-plus-infinitive* construction. In other words, *teacher* is the direct object of the verb *to want* and the verb that expresses the action of the teacher is left in the infinitive—*to explain*. In Spanish, on the other hand, there are two clauses: each doer of an action gets his or her own conjugated verb. Let's take a look at the structure of this previous Spanish sentence in an abstract form, as if it were a chemical or mathematical formula.

$$S_1 + V_1 \text{ que } S_2 + V_2$$

Still, how will you know a subordinated noun clause to be a subordinated *noun* clause and not some other type of subordinated clause? In other words, what makes it a noun clause? Remember, a subordinated noun clause is a large direct object. A direct object is always a *noun* or a word that stands in for one. Anything that acts like a noun could be substituted for a noun, so we can create a sort of a litmus test by having a handy word to use, a neutral word, like *chocolate*. Let's see how this idea works.

Deseo **chocolate**.

*I want **chocolate**.*

This obviously creates a perfect sentence, but sometimes a slight adjustment has to be made, depending on the verb in the main clause.

Espero **chocolate**.

*I hope for **chocolate**.*

Adding the preposition *for* is not cheating because in Spanish it is understood after **pedir**, **esperar**, and **buscar**. Using a word such as *chocolate* for the entire subordinated clause allowed you to determine if the result was grammatical, and therefore the clause was a subordinated noun clause. Now we get *I hope for chocolate*, a great sentence! In like manner, since we can substitute **que el maestro explique el subjuntivo** with the noun **chocolate** and create a grammatical sentence, **Deseo chocolate**, we can conclude that the clause beginning with **que** is a subordinated noun clause and not some other type of clause.

Identifying the clause as a noun clause supplies the information needed for the next step in which you will apply the rules for the use of the subjunctive when dealing with a subordinated noun clause. Now you're ready for the rule that will enable you to determine whether the verb in such clauses needs to be in the subjunctive. Remember that in the exercises that follow, you'll also have to remember the principles involved in order to determine *which* of the four possible tenses of the subjunctive you'll need.

The rule is that V_2 *must be in the subjunctive form if and only if there is a change of subject, that is, if S_1 and S_2 are not the same person and if V_1 is a W.E.I.R.D.O. verb.*

Now, W.E.I.R.D.O. is a nifty little acronym that stands for all the lists of verbs you may have been carrying around on scraps or reams of paper, or worse yet, on napkins from the student cafeteria, trying to memorize when to use the subjunctive. Instead of mentally running through all those lists and risking coffee spills that can obliterate an afternoon's hard work, you need only have a decent verb vocabulary and powers of classification. When using a verb in the main clause, and following it with a subordinate clause, you need only classify the main verb to determine if the subjunctive is required in the second clause. Memorize the following economical acronym—and it can't be spoiled by coffee spills. The categories of verbs encompassed by V_1 include the following:

W A verb of **w**ishing, willing, wanting, hoping, expecting, etc.

E A verb or **e**motion (note: most of these verbs are reflexive)

I An **i**mpersonal expression of W.E.R.D., introduced by **es** + *adjective*; a verb or other expression that expresses influence

R A verb of **r**equesting, asking, demanding, commanding, or causing

D A verb of **d**oubt, denial, or negation

O *Ojalá* (**que**—which may be omitted when using this word)

Now, let's translate the formula $S_1 + V_1$ **que** $S_2 + V_2$ into prose, so you can memorize it easily:

If $S_1 \neq S_2$ and if V_1 is a W.E.I.R.D.O. verb, then V_2 will have to be in the subjunctive.

That's it. Otherwise, V_2 will not be subjunctive. Not ever. If there is no change of grammatical subject (the *doer* of the two actions), then there is no need to form a subordinated clause.

Queremos **ir** a la tienda.	*We want **to go** to the store.*

For instance, in this example, the subject of the main clause, *we*, is also the understood subject of *go*. English and Spanish handle this the same way grammatically. Both languages use a helping verb—in this case *to want*—plus a *complementary infinitive*, in this case, *to go*. Just as the name denotes, the complementary infinitive is complementary because it *completes* the idea introduced by the helping verb.

Note that with verbs of doubt and emotion, this is not always observed:

Dudo que yo pueda ir.	*I doubt that I will be able to go.*

Many speakers, more conscious of style, form, and grammar, prefer to use a complementary infinitive when there is no change of subject from the main clause to the subordinate clause:

Dudo poder ir.	*I doubt that I will be able to go.*

Some books add a third condition for when the subjunctive might be needed, and that is if **que** is used. But this is simply not true, because the use of **que** is not causal in any way. The truth is that **que** is used to introduce subordinated clauses of *all* kinds, whether or not they require the subjunctive. Another weakness with this misleading third rule is that it conditions students to be passive, to merely look for **que** on the next quiz or midterm, close their eyes, and scribble their best version of the subjunctive in the next blank. No! You're smarter than that! Remember that **que** is simply grammatical glue, a connective (called a *conjunction*), used in many situations. Its presence here is in no way *causative* of the subjunctive. The *type* of verb in the V_1 position, however, plus the *change of subject*, *are* causative.

The verb in the V₁ position is always in the indicative. It may seem at first glance that this rule does not apply to indirect commands, but it does, as the following examples will show, because the verb of wanting is simply suppressed, or understood. Of course, the English translations cannot do justice to the structure, but this is, in effect, what is happening.

¡Que Susana no me hable!	*Don't let Susan speak to me!*
Yo quiero que Susana no me hable.	*I want Susan to not speak to me.*

Following are some examples of sentences whose main clauses contain W.E.I.R.D.O. verbs, and whose verbs in their subordinated noun clauses, therefore, all must be in the subjunctive form. The sentences are arranged in W.E.I.R.D.O. order:

Quiero que Juan venga a la fiesta.	*I **want** John to come to the party.*
Me alegro de que Juan venga a la fiesta.	*I **am glad** John is coming to the party.*
Es importante que Juan venga a la fiesta.	*It **is important** for John to come to the party.*
Vamos a **pedir**le que venga a la fiesta.	*Let's **ask** him to come to the party.*
Dudo que Juan venga a la fiesta.	*I **doubt** that John will come to the party.*
¡**Ojalá** que venga Juan a la fiesta!	*I **hope to God** John comes to the party!*

Let's take a good look at the **D** category, the one representing verbs of *doubt*, since it is the category that seems to infect too many other areas of understanding of the rules about, and application of, the subjunctive in various situations. First of all, as was stated earlier, whether people believe or disbelieve things has little connection with whether the things are true or not. Second, although belief itself is not a certainty, in Spanish, verbs in subordinated clauses introduced by main clauses containing *assertions of belief* will have the verb in that subordinated clause expressed with the indicative. More traditional experts in style recommend that the subjunctive be used in subordinated clauses introduced even by verbs of belief—when asking a question. Take a look at the following examples:

Tú **crees** que la fiesta **es** hoy.	*You **believe** that the party **is** today.*
Nosotros **dudamos** que la fiesta **sea** hoy.	*We **doubt** that the party **is** today.*
¿**Crees** tú que la fiesta **vaya a empezar** pronto?	*Do you **believe** that the party **is going to start** soon?*

It is critical to realize from these last examples that the requirement to use subjunctive or indicative has nothing to do with whether you or we are right or wrong. The use of the subjunctive or the indicative depends only on whether all the conditions that could require its use are met. Whether the result is that the subjunctive or the indicative has to be used, it is irrelevant whether you or we are wrong now, or turn out to be wrong later. The fact is, in the first sentence, your belief is asserted and V₂ is in the *indicative*. In the second, our disbelief is expressed and V₂ is in the *subjunctive*.

If instead, the main clause is negated in each case and changed to **Tú no crees** and **Nosotros no dudamos**, the use of indicative and the subjunctive in the subordinated clauses is reversed.

Tú **no crees** que la fiesta **sea** hoy.	You **don't believe** that the party **is** today.
Nosotros **no dudamos** que la fiesta **es** hoy.	We **don't doubt** that the party **is** today.

Thus, for grammatical purposes, when you negate a denial or a disbelief, it is viewed as a positive statement; therefore, the indicative is used in the subordinated clause. Conversely, and again for grammatical purposes only, if you negate a belief, a statement of doubt is created, and therefore the subjunctive is used in that sentence's subordinated noun clause. Also note that in the English translation, there is no change in verb form in the subordinated clause—the principal cause of confusion for English speakers being that the subjunctive is rendered invisible in translation and therefore seems unnecessary.

The exercise sets from this point on in this book will require you not only to determine whether the subjunctive is needed, but if so, which one. If it is not needed, and a conjugated verb is needed, you will still need to make a proper choice of tense. The next sets deal strictly with subordinated noun clauses—or situations in which there may be no subordinated noun clause and therefore require a complementary infinitive or perhaps an indicative form, in any variety of tenses.

EJERCICIO
3·1

Fill in the blanks using the proper form of the verbs in parentheses.

1. Es bueno que Juan _piense_ mucho en ella. (pensar)

2. Me fue obvio que ellas _hablaban_ en voz baja cuando entré en el cuarto. (hablar)

3. Esperábamos que tú _vieras_ la película ayer. (ver)

4. Me alegro de que Uds. _vengan_ a la fiesta hoy. (venir)

5. Ella duda que Juan _vaya_ al cine. (ir)

6. Tú dudas que yo _pueda_ comer todo el pastel. (poder)

7. Juan me pidió que _alquilara_ su apartamento el verano pasado. (alquilar)

8. No creemos que Juan _haya vivido_ jamás en el Japón. (vivir)

9. Dudamos que la policía _pueda_ identificarlo. (poder)

10. Pídale que _traduzca_ el documento. (traducir)

11. Es dudoso que tú y Juan _sepan_ arreglar motocicletas. (saber)

12. Mi amigo creía que ella _llevaba_ un vestido muy bello anoche. (llevar)

Matching. Select the clauses on the right that both logically and grammatically finish the sentences begun by the independent clauses on the left.

1. _h_ Los profesores esperan...

2. _b_ En la fiesta, yo no quería...

3. _a_ Para la luna de miel, ella insistió en...

4. _c_ En caso de incendio, es urgente...

5. _f_ En un restaurante, yo pido...

6. _g_ Su padre le recomienda a Juan...

7. _c_ Los agnósticos dudan...

8. _j_ Una persona religiosa cree...

9. _d_ Hace buen tiempo y me alegro de...

10. _i_ De noche, muchos niños temen...

a. ... que fueran a Acapulco.

b. ... que ellas me invitaran a bailar.

c. ... que Dios exista.

d. ... poder tomar el sol.

e. ... llamar a los bomberos.

f. ... que el mesero me traiga el menú.

g. ... que estudie negocios.

h. ... que los estudiantes aprendan.

i. ... dormir sin una luz encendida.

j. ... que Dios existe.

Multiple choice. Write the letter of the dependent noun clause that correctly completes the sentence.

1. Nuestro jefe nos pide _____.
   a. que trabajáramos de noche
   b. quedarnos a trabajar de noche
   c. que trabajemos de noche
   d. que trabajamos de noche

2. La mayoría de los ciudadanos no querían _____.
   a. que se contruye una carretera por ahí
   b. que haya más escuelas primarias en la ciudad
   c. que contrataran a más empleados administrativos
   d. que cobran más impuestos

3. La secretaria del bufete de abogados insistía en _____.
   a. que ellos le entregan sus documentos todos los días
   b. que ellos mantuvieran sus expedientes cronológicos de manera organizada
   c. que ellos echen los documentos a la basura
   d. que ellos enviaron la documentación por correo aéreo

4. Cuando leía el periódico sobre los políticos, me molestó _____.
   a. que uno hubiera sobornado a un juez
   b. que unos han sobornado a un juez
   c. que alguien soborne a un juez
   d. que sobornan a los jueces

5. Mi amigo Lorenzo cree _____.
   a. que él se divierta en la Via Appia más que nadie
   b. que él se divierte en la Via Appia más que nadie
   c. divertirse en la Via Appia más que nadie
   d. que todos se diviertan en la Via Appia más que él

6. Susana no quería _____.
   a. que los administradores me eximieran de sus falsos cargos
   b. que el decano está de acuerdo conmigo
   c. que yo trabajo como profesor
   d. que mi jefa me defiende

7. El gerente de la compañía les pide a sus empleados _____.
   a. que salían más temprano todos los días
   c. que mejoren su rendimiento
   d. que evalúan su desempeño en el trabajo
   b. que emplearon prácticas más modernas
   c. que mejoren su rendimiento
   d. que evalúan su desempeño en el trabajo

8. Cuando la señora fue al fotógrafo, él le dijo _____.
   a. que no mira directamente a la cámara
   b. que no le guste su maquillaje
   c. mirar directamente a la cámara
   d. que no le hablara tanto porque esto lo distraía

9. El detective espera _____.
   a. que la evidencia verifica sus sospechas
   b. que la evidencia verificaba sus sospechas
   c. que la evidencia verifique sus sospechas
   d. que la evidencia verificó sus sospechas

10. Los turistas veían _____.
    a. que el restaurante abriera a las ocho de la mañana
    b. que las tiendas abrían a las ocho de la mañana
    c. que el restaurante abra a las ocho de la mañana
    d. que las tiendas abrieron a las ocho de la mañana

EJERCICIO
3·4

Translate the following sentences from Spanish into English.

1. Es importante darle las noticias a Juan lo antes posible.

   It is important to give John the news as soon as possible.

2. Nuestros padres esperaban que nosotros tuviéramos éxito en la vida.

   Our parents hoped we would be successful in life.

3. Diles que no vayan a esa playa porque hay mucha contaminación.

   Tell them not to go to that beach because its polluted.

4. Era preciso que ellos sirvieran la comida a tiempo.

   It was imperative that they serve the food on time

5. Dudo que tú sepas mucho sobre la astronomía de los babilonios.

I doubt that you know much about Babylonian astronomy.

6. No creíamos que ella hubiera estudiado la lección antes de venir a clase.

We did not believe tha she had studied the lesson before coming to class.

7. Los médicos nos recomiendan que durmamos por lo menos siete horas.

Doctors recomend thatget at least seven hours of sleep

8. Va a ser muy importante que tú puedas usar el subjuntivo si quieres ir a México.

It's going to be very important for you to be able to use the subjuctive If you want to go to mexico.

9. Ella dudaba que él quisiera que ella lo acompañara a la fiesta.

She doubted that he wanted her to go with him to the party

10. No podía creer que Susana me hubiera investigado antes de pedirme la lista.

I could not believe that Susan had investigated me before asking me for the list

EJERCICIO
3·5

Translate the following sentences from English into Spanish.

1. Her friends asked her to bring her digital camera to the party.

Sus amigos le pidieron que trajera su cámara digital a la fiesta.

2. We were hoping she would find a new boyfriend.

Esperabamos que ella consiguiera un nuevo novio.

3. They wanted him to leave.

Ellos querían que él se fuera.

4. Do you hope the opera will start soon? (use the **tú** form for *you*)

¿Esperas que la Opera comience pronto?

5. Her parents are glad that she has married Matthew.

Sus Padres se alegran de que ella se haya casado con Mateo.

6. Is it necessary that we pay for the food here?

¿Es necesario que se pague la comida aquí?

7. Her bosses expected her to tape all the phone calls.

Sus jefes esperaban que ella grababa todas las llamadas telefónicas.

8. The police asked the people to look for the lost dog.

La policía pidio que se buscava el perro perdido.

9. Are you glad that she went to Europe?

¿Te alegras de que ella se haya ido a Europa?

10. Were they angry that she had returned early?

¿Se enojaron de que ella hubiera vuelto temprano?

Fill in the blanks in the following paragraph using the list of verbs below. Some will be needed more than once.

acusar	dudar	haber
ofender	respaldar	ser
castigar	enfadar	obligar
ponerse	saber	pedir
tener		

Yo (1) __me puse__ furioso cuando (2) __supe__ cómo, antes de

solicitarme una lista de mis publicaciones y sin pedirme explicaciones, Susana se

(3) __hubiera__ tomado el trabajo de investigarme a mis espaldas. Me

(4) __enfadó__ que me (5) __hubiera__ denunciado ante los

administradores, diciendo que yo (6) __había__ falsificado mi currículum vitae. Era el colmo. Yo (7) _dudaba_ que los jefes me (8) _respaldaran_

porque ella les (9) _había_ declarado que sus sospechas

(10) _eran_ ciertas. Me (11) _enfadó_ que me (12) _acusara_

simplemente con preguntas acusatorias y que ellos jamás le (13) _obligaran_

a probarlas. En efecto, las preguntas (14) _eran_ ataques basados en

mentiras y motivados por su rencor contra mí. No obstante, yo (15) _tenía_

toda la documentación necesaria para probar que no (16) _había_ sido

deshonesto en ningún momento. Lo más insultante de todo esto fue que aun

entonces, ellos no le (17) _castigaran_ por cómo ella me (18) _había_

maltratado y que ni me (19) _pidieran_ disculpas.

Subordinated adjective clauses

Remember how you determined whether a subordinated clause was a noun clause or not by substituting a noun? Well, there is a similar test for adjective clauses. Can you guess what it is? Right, you'll make a similar substitution or stand-in word as a litmus test, only you'll substitute an *adjective* instead of a noun. You could use any adjective you like, but in our first example, we'll use the word **cobarde**; since it ends in an **-e**, it isn't inflected to show gender. In the case of plurals, add an **-s** to make it plural.

It is important to understand and keep in mind that the W.E.I.R.D.O. rule *only* applies to determining whether you need the subjunctive in the subordinated *noun* clauses. The rule that we are going to explore in this unit is that the subjunctive is used in a subordinated *adjective* clause when that clause modifies an indefinite, vague, or nonexistent (unreal) *antecedent*. Once you have determined that you are dealing with an *adjective* clause, you can apply the rule to determine whether the subjunctive is needed or not.

An *antecedent* is a previously mentioned noun, which is the understood or implied subject of the verb in the adjective clause. The clause refers back to and describes this previously mentioned noun. In the following example, the word *computer* is the *antecedent* of the subordinated adjective clause *that works*.

> Necesitamos una computadora **que funcione**. *We need a computer **that works**.*

Just as was the case with subordinated noun clauses, we have a main clause followed by **que**. The verb **necesitamos** (*we need*), with its direct object noun, **una computadora**, form the main clause. So far, this structure looks identical to what we have already seen with noun clauses, but in the remainder of this sentence, the structure and its function will be different. Note that the direct object of that verb is *a computer*. As with all direct objects, it explains *what* we need. The subordinated clause is easily identified as that part of the sentence that begins with **que**, just as with subordinated noun clauses, but in this case, there are two differences. First, *computer* is the subject of the verb of the subordinated clause, *to work*. Second, *computer* is not stated as the subject of the subordinated clause, but rather is implicit, or understood in context.

The grammatical subject can be omitted from subordinated noun clauses as well, and when it is, the two types of subordinated clauses can be deceptively similar. That is why the litmus test is needed to determine what sort of clause the subordinated clause is.

Applying the litmus test using *cowardly*, we see that *We need a computer cowardly* doesn't form a standard English sentence, but this is only because of English word order. Placing the word *cowardly* before the noun in English remedies that difficulty. You can easily see that *cowardly* creates a grammatically correct sentence, even if it is a bit silly, because it is used as an adjective. It works perfectly in Spanish also, as you can tell.

Necesitamos una computadora **cobarde**.   *We need a **cowardly** computer.*

Another way to test the adjective clause is to turn the clause itself into a single adjective that means the same thing as the clause. This is an easy procedure, particularly if the clause is not too long.

Necesitamos una computadora **funcional**.   *We need a **working** computer.*

Sometimes the sentences that result from these litmus tests are surreal and even kind of fun, but they will make the clause type stand out instantly. If you prefer to use a different adjective, such as **interesante**, you can, of course, but it is a good idea to use one that ends in an **-e**, for reasons explained previously.

To build confidence in this substitution technique, let's confirm that when applied to subordinated noun clauses, it will not create grammatically correct sentences. A misclassification would lead you to incorrectly apply the W.E.I.R.D.O. rule. This time, let's use **interesante** to see if it can effectively stand in as a substitute for what we suspect is an adjective clause.

Me alegro de **que no llueva hoy**.   I'm glad *that it isn't raining today*.
*Me alegro de **interesante**.   *I'm glad *interesting*.

Es importante **que tú traigas el paraguas**.   It's important *that you bring your umbrella*.
*Es importante **interesante**.   *It's important *interesting*.

The resulting sentences, both Spanish and English, are obviously ungrammatical and have been marked as such with an asterisk.

It never hurts to apply both the noun and adjective litmus tests to sentences you hear, read, say, or write, so that between the two, you can be confident with your determination and proceed to apply the correct rule to determine whether or not you need to use the subjunctive in the subordinated clause. Once again, you can pick your own favorite nouns and adjectives. For nouns, **papel** and **árbol** are often effective. For adjectives, colors are good, especially **azul** and **verde**. After a bit of practice, you'll be sensitized to the difference between noun clauses and adjective clauses and you'll be able to abandon these verbal training wheels.

There are a few other fine adjustments that need to be made in order to build this sensitivity. Sometimes it helps to observe whether the article before the antecedent is *definite* (**el**, **la**, **los**, or **las**) or *indefinite* (**un**, **una**, **unos**, or **unas**). This is a helpful hint, but it is *not* always true. In the examples below, notice how, when the *indefinite* article is used, the verb in the subordinated noun clause may or may not be in the subjunctive. The determining factor is the verb of the main clause—whether it denotes having something as opposed to needing or searching for something. When the *definite* article is used, the *indicative* will be used because the function of a definite article is to indicate something specific.

Necesitamos una computadora que **funcione**.	We **need a** computer that works.
Tenemos una computadora que **funciona**.	We **have a** computer that works.
Necesitamos **la** computadora que **funciona**.	We need **the** computer that works.

Finally, when the main clause asserts that the antecedent doesn't exist, the subjunctive must be used in the subordinated adjective clause. This situation is an excellent example to refute the often repeated idea about the subjunctive—that it is all about uncertainty.

No hay ninguna computadora aquí que **funcione**.	*There isn't one* computer here that works.

Sometimes, students report having been told by their teachers to observe whether the *personal* **a** (the means by which a noun is marked as object, not subject, to eliminate ambiguity) is used or not before antecedents referring to people in the main clause, with the advice that when an antecedent is indefinite or vague, the *personal* **a** is not used. In addition to encouraging passivity (it sounds like test-taking advice), no such rule exists. The *personal* **a** is frequently omitted after certain common verbs that introduce human direct objects that, as antecedents, may be vague or not. Most important, an example of the subjunctive used in an adjective clause in the *Gramática de la lengua española* of the Real Academia de la Lengua (1928 edition, p. 369) employs not only the definite article but the *personal* **a** as well:

Prefiero **a los** niños que **sean** dóciles.	*I prefer children who are manageable.*

This authoritative example demonstrates that the alleged omission of the *personal* **a** before vague antecedents and the subjunctive in the following adjective clauses modifying them are separate issues, even if they occasionally do cross paths. The fact that the *personal* **a** can be omitted after some common verbs seems to account for the misinterpretation by some teachers.

In a nutshell, the use or nonuse of the *personal* **a** isn't what *causes* the indicative or the subjunctive to be required. What causes the subjunctive to be required is the vagueness of the antecedent in the speaker's mind or an assertion that it does not exist.

Finally, some advice about speaking. Be especially careful to *not* put stress on the endings, whether it is an effort to impress upon your own mind or a listener's that you are aware of the difference between the subjunctive and the indicative. Pronounce vowels so purely that there is no mistake about which one it is, regardless of whether they are stressed or not. The stress rules are unaffected by whether the verb ends in an **-a** or an **-e**. Stressing a final syllable can lead to major confusion, as can be seen in the difference between the first- or third-person singular of the present subjunctive, **hable**, and the first-person singular of the preterite, **hablé**.

EJERCICIO
4·1

Fill in the blanks, using either the present indicative, present subjunctive, imperfect indicative, imperfect subjunctive, or preterite indicative of the verbs in parentheses.

1. No hay ningún político allí que ___sea___ honesto. (ser)

2. Buscamos una maleta que no ___tenga___ ese defecto. (tener)

3. ¿Hay alguien que ___sepa___ hacer *pollo a la Kiev*? (saber)

4. Él tenía una secretaria que ___escribía___ rápido. (escribir)

5. El coro buscaba una cantante que ___cantara___ arias italianas. (cantar)

6. Yo quería un asistente que ___pudiera___ manejar los detalles de mi compañía. (poder)

7. No hay nadie en ese banco que ___vaya___ a abrir la caja hoy. (ir)

8. Quiero hablar con el señor que le ___entregó___ el paquete. (entregar)

9. Necesitábamos alguien que ___tradujera___ documentos técnicos. (traducir)

10. No hay ningún concierto aquí que ___empiece___ antes de las ocho. (empezar)

11. Fue preciso comprar un televisor que ___tuviera___ buena recepción. (tener)

12. Ellos desean encontrar puestos que ___paguen___ bien después de graduarse. (pagar)

Matching. Select the clauses on the right that both logically and grammatically finish the sentences begun by the independent clauses on the left.

1. __f__ Deseábamos hallar un hotel...

2. __e__ Susana no pudo hallar un novio...

3. __i__ Juan busca un carro...

4. __j__ Buscaron al periodista...

5. __a__ ¿Necesitas ir de vacaciones...

6. __d__ Teníamos una casa...

7. __h__ Prefieren hablar con personas...

8. __g__ Había una estatua en el pueblo...

9. __c__ ¿Hay una tienda cerca de aquí...

10. __b__ Tenemos un perro...

a. ... a un lugar en que haga mucho sol?

b. ... que sabe hacer muchos trucos.

c. ... en que se vendan camisas de seda?

d. ... que tenía tres niveles.

e. ... que se atreviera a casarse con ella.

f. ... que tuviera aire acondicionado.

g. ... que era de una persona famosa.

h. ... que sepan mucho sobre el arte.

i. ... que no use tanta gasolina.

j. ... que escribió sobre escándalos políticos.

Multiple choice. Write the letter of the dependent adjective clause that correctly completes the sentence.

1. El candidato esperaba hallar a más personas _____.
   a. que son talentosas
   b. que tienen dinero en el banco para contribuir a su campaña
   c. quienes pudieran ser convencidas a estar de acuerdo con él antes de las elecciones
   d. que pueden hablar muchas lenguas para ayudarle en su campaña política

2. Esas secretarias se quejaban de aquellos jefes _____.
   a. que no les permitieran pasar más tiempo con sus familias
   b. que trabajan mucho
   c. que se vestían de manera ridícula
   d. que son ricos

3. No me gusta besar a una persona _____.
   a. que tiene dientes amarillos
   b. que huela a tabaco
   c. que no sonríe
   d. que solamente piensa en sí misma

4. Casanova prefería a las mujeres _____.
   a. que saben bailar bien
   b. que conocieran el mundo
   c. que bailen bien
   d. que hablan francés

5. Los miembros del equipo esperan tener un entrenador _____.
   a. que es de Alemania
   b. que sabía las reglas del juego
   c. que supo todo sobre el béisbol
   d. que sepa más sobre la fisiología de los deportes

6. Los novios buscan un libro de gastronomía _____.
   a. que incluye recetas españolas
   b. que incluya recetas de España
   c. que incluía recetas de España
   d. que incluyan recetas españolas

7. Sus padres querían enviarla a una universidad _____.
   a. en que no se les permitía tomar cerveza
   b. que ofrece muchas especializaciones
   c. en que fuera prohibido tomar bebidas alcohólicas
   d. que tiene un programa de negocios

8. Las niñas buscan la muñeca _____.
   a. que llora y habla
   b. que llorara y hablara
   c. que llore y hable
   d. que lloran y hablan

9. No había ningún lago allí _____.
   a. que tienen muchos peces
   b. que no fuera contaminado
   c. en que no se ven otros pescadores
   d. que son grandes y profundos

10. ¿Prefieres una novela _____?
   a. que se compra en el supermercado
   b. en que el héroe siempre se case con la heroína
   c. que trata de temas góticos
   d. que tiene lugar en islas del mar Caribe

EJERCICIO
4·4

Translate the following sentences from Spanish to English.

1. Los ingenieros necesitaban hallar una solución que no fuera tan costosa.

_____

2. Preferíamos escuchar música que no nos pusiera nerviosos.

_____

3. Los músicos tienen guitarras que suenan bien.

_____

4. La astronauta quería tener un novio que le fuera fiel.

_____

5. No hay ropa de esos diseñadores que sea práctica.

_____

6. No me interesan los libros que se venden en el cajero del supermercado.

_____

7. Un día esperamos vivir en una casa que tenga un garaje grande.

_____

8. Deseaba comprar un barco de velas que pudiera navegar muy rápido.

_____

9. No hay hombre que iguale a Don Juan en juegos, en lid o en amores.

_____

10. Tengo una linterna que ilumina un gran trecho del camino.

_____

EJERCICIO
4·5

Translate the following sentences from English to Spanish.

1. They needed a table that was bigger.

   Necesitaban una mesa que fuera mas grande

2. We want to find a city that has less crime.

   Queremos hallar una ciudad que tenga menos crimen.

3. There wasn't a guy there who didn't like sports.

   No había ni un muchacho ahí a quien no le gustaran los deportes.

4. He and I were looking for a dictionary that included mechanical terms.

   _____

5. I want a garden that has all blue flowers.

   _____

6. He wants to vote for the candidate who has the best ideas.

   _____

7. He hopes to find a candidate who is honest.

   _____

8. They were looking for a map that showed the parks.

   _____

9. Do you want to go to a beach that has picnic tables?

   _____

10. We found a used car that had new tires.

    _____

Adverbial expressions

For many language learners, memorization poses a serious challenge. Some textbooks offer shorter lists of the adverbial expressions you are about to see, perhaps in an effort to make memorization less burdensome, but at the expense of completeness.

In the case of the adverbial expressions, the whole story may be told without making unreasonable demands on your powers of memorization. In this case, the dividends of your efforts will come quickly. After you have memorized list **A**, the list of expressions after which the subjunctive must *always* be used, you'll be glad to discover that there's only one rule to determine whether or not the subjunctive must be used after the adverbial expressions in list **B**. It is a good idea to commit list **B** to memory as well. When using an expression from list **B**, there is only one rule to resolve your doubts and determine whether to use or not use the subjunctive with adverbial expressions.

This time, there's no acronym or word as a litmus test to see if you're dealing with an adverbial clause or not because the phrases you'll memorize are *all* adverbial. Instead of a litmus test using a substitute word for a clause, the decision to use or not use the subjunctive after those adverbial expressions that could be followed by the subjunctive or the indicative depends on a key temporal concept—anticipation. You should consider *anticipation* to be the key word when deliberating about needing the subjunctive with adverbial expressions. Learning to recognize the element of anticipation in the context of the whole sentence will enable you to tip the balance when deliberating about whether to use the subjunctive or not after an expression in list **B**. Note that most of the expressions in list **B** involve or imply some explicit reference to *time*.

List A: "Always" adverbial expressions

Always use the subjunctive after these expressions:

a menos que, a no ser que	*unless*
antes de que	*before*
como si	*as if*
con tal de que, siempre y cuando	*provided that, as long as*
el hecho de que	*the fact that*
en caso de que	*in case (that)*
para que, a fin de que	*in order that*
sin que	*without*

A couple of observations about two expressions in the above list are necessary at this point, and should simply be noted as rules of the road, as footnotes in your memory. First, after the expression **como si**, only the *imperfect subjunctive* or *pluperfect subjunctive* must be used. The choice follows the rules for sequence of tenses that you have seen.

Ese chico corre como si **naciera** para ello.	*That kid runs as if he **were born** for it.*
Ese chico corría como si **hubiera nacido** para ello.	*That kid ran as if he **had been born** for it.*

Second, you may find the indicative after the expression **el hecho de que**, but the reasoning in support of stylistic experts' preference for the use of the subjunctive after this expression is that it is often used in situations in which the speaker implies doubt and that it is essentially an ironic statement.

El hecho de que Juana **venga** no me anima a ir también.	*The fact that Juana **may come** does not encourage me to go also.*
El hecho de que Juana **viniera** no me animaba a ir también.	*The fact that Juana **might have been coming** did not encourage me to go also.*

Even in cases when a speaker or writer wishes to assert certainty, the subjunctive is grammatically correct. In both the following examples, the speaker is certain that Juana either *has come* or *came*. In the second example, the insertion of the word **efectivamente** has been used to show that the certainty of the speaker does not mitigate the need to use the subjunctive.

El hecho de que Juana **haya venido** no me anima a ir también.	*The fact that Juana **has come** does not encourage me to go also.*
El hecho de que Juana efectivamente **viniera** no me animaba a ir también.	*The fact that Juana definitely **came** did not encourage me to go also.*

List B: "Sometimes" adverbial expressions

The subjunctive is *sometimes* used after these expressions:

a pesar de que	*despite, in spite of*
acaso, tal vez, quizá	*perhaps*
así que, así como	*such that*
aunque	*although*
cuando	*when*
de modo que, de manera que	*in such a way that*
después de que, luego que	*after*
hasta que	*until*
mientras	*while*
por más que, por mucho que	*no matter how much*
siempre que	*as long as*
tan pronto como, en cuanto	*as soon as*
una vez que	*once you have*

Of the expressions in the **B** list, the word **aunque** offers some opportunities to understand the subjunctive, to get inside its logic, but they can be deceptive, just as the concept of doubt can overshadow the whole topic when it is introduced in the context of the subordinated noun clauses. In the case of **aunque**, it is an example of how the use of the indicative or the subjunctive truly depends *entirely* on the attitude—or degree of confidence—a speaker has about his or her assertion.

In English, speakers often employ voice stress to show doubt. By using their voice, they can convey their attitude or degree of conviction or certainty, either with or without using *may*. In Spanish, however, the indicative or subjunctive is used, respectively, to communicate these attitudes and degrees of conviction, regardless of tone, and often without much difference in tone. Thus, a degree of certitude is communicated by the use of the indicative *alone*, regardless of stress. In English, the verb is stressed to show this assertion, because it lacks a subjunctive form to perform that communicative function.

> Aunque Juan **es** rico, no lo parece.   *Even though John **is** rich, he doesn't seem to be.*

Similarly, in English, *may* is used to express doubts or the possibility that one's impressions could be wrong. The word *may* alone is enough to indicate one's doubts, but many speakers still stress it for emphasis. In Spanish, there is no need to add voice stress and few would, even for emphasis.

> Aunque Juan **sea** rico, no lo parece.   *Although Juan **may** be rich, he doesn't seem to be.*

Turning our attention to the **A** list, you'll notice that the only expression of *time* on this list is **antes de que**. This anomaly provides an opportunity to understand how the key word *anticipation* functions when deliberating over the use of the subjunctive after expressions on the **B** list. Let's go step-by-step to see what makes **antes de que** so different from the other time expressions, found on the **B** list, that it should end up on the **A** list. We will use a contrastive approach, comparing **antes de que** with its opposite, **después de que**, *after*.

The first clue is found in the meanings of these two expressions themselves, *before* on the one hand, *after* on the other. Next, consider the fact that the action expressed by *any* verb following the word *before* can never have occurred already. When you studied sequence of tenses, you learned that the temporal point of reference is provided by the main verb of the sentence in which it appears. This will be very important in order to appreciate the contrasting examples below, from the days before cellphones!

In the first example below, Juan's call is anticipated. The speaker states that he will go to the movies only after he gets the call from Juan. The subjunctive is required now, not because of any attitude on the part of the speaker, but strictly because of the element of anticipation at the moment the speaker utters the sentence.

> Yo iré al cine después de que Juan me **llame**.   *I'll go to the movies after John calls me.*

However, as the following example shows, if the speaker is reporting what happened yesterday, the element of anticipation is absent at the moment of the utterance. Therefore, the indicative must be used.

> Yo fui al cine después de que Juan me **llamó**.   *I went to the movies after John called me.*

Next, let's examine why the subjunctive *must* be used after **antes de que**, whether it is introduced by a present, future, or past tense verb. In the first of the following two examples, Juan's call can't have been made yet. It is anticipated. The speaker is leaving the house and Juan may call after that. Maybe the speaker doesn't want to talk to him or doesn't have time to wait for the call. The reasons are irrelevant. What makes the call *anticipated* from the temporal perspective of the moment of the utterance is that the speaker is leaving before the phone can ring.

> Yo iré al cine antes de que Juan me **llame**.   *I'll go to the movies before John calls me.*

In the following example, note how shifting this situation to a prior time does not change the relationship between the speaker's leaving the house and the time of the phone call, from the temporal point of view of the moment that the speaker refers to. Juan's call had not been made at the time the speaker claims he left, and so the call was, at that moment, *anticipated*. The speaker reports that he left the house; whether Juan called, left a message, or didn't call at all is irrelevant. The only thing that matters is that at the time the speaker left, the call was anticipated and therefore the subjunctive is required.

Yo fui al teatro antes de que Juan me **llamara**.	*I went to the movies before John called me.*

Regardless of the type of adverbial expression, remember that if there is no clause (i.e., **que** is not used to introduce a conjugated verb), then an infinitive will follow the preposition. Learners of Spanish are often happy to learn rules with a 100 percent reliability, especially if the contrasting English situation also has a one-to-one correlation. In English, the verb form that must follow a preposition is the gerund, or *-ing* form; in Spanish, it is always the infinitive. In both languages, this is because there is no change of subject for the two actions in the sentence. In the following sentence, the children are the subject of the verbs **bañarse** (*to bathe*) and **acostarse** (*to go to bed*).

Los chicos se bañaron antes de **acostarse**.	*The children bathed before **going** to bed.*

Before proceeding to the exercises, be sure you are secure about the concept of the sequence of tenses. In addition, if the forms of the subjunctive continue to be a problem for you, it is probably because you still are a bit rusty with the present and preterite indicative. Be sure to continually review these tenses, comparing the formation of the present subjunctive from the first-person singular (**yo**) form of the present indicative and the formation of the imperfect subjunctive from the third-person plural (**Uds.**, **ellos**, **ellas**) of the preterite.

EJERCICIO
5·1

Fill in the blanks with the proper form of the verb in parentheses. Remember, any tense could be necessary. From now on, one blank may require more than one word, so watch out for reflexive verbs and compound tenses.

1. Ellos no soltaron ni un centavo, hasta que su tío _____ en la Bolsa y se ganó un millón de dólares. (invertir)

2. Yo iré contigo, con tal de que tú _____ el auto a tiempo. (vender)

3. No van a ganar nada, aunque _____ a mil expertos. (contratar)

4. Salimos para el aeropuerto anoche antes de que mamá _____ las cajas. (empacar)

5. El juez pondrá en libertad al periodista tan pronto como le _____ quién le reveló la información inflamatoria. (decir)

6. Fuimos al cine despúes de que el mesero nos _____ la cuenta. (traer)

7. Podremos ir al zoológico cuando los niños _____ los zapatos. (ponerse)

8. No votaré por un candidato a menos que yo lo _____ personalmente. (conocer)

9. El abogado llevaba los documentos como si los _____ en una bandeja de cristal. (traer)

10. Los niños jugaban en casa con cuidado para no _____ los muebles. (romper)

11. Fuimos al teatro antes de que _____ la llamada de nuestra tía. (recibir)

12. Anoche, llamamos a nuestro socio antes de _____ el paquete con las muestras. (enviar)

EJERCICIO

5·2

Matching. Select the clauses on the right that both logically and grammatically finish the sentences begun on the left.

1. _____ Ella se pone loción en caso de que...

2. _____ El chico salió cuando...

3. _____ El gato corre como si...

4. _____ Voy a subir la montaña tan pronto como...

5. _____ Juan salió de casa sin que...

6. _____ El joven la espera aunque...

a. ... vayas a Roma, haz como ellos.

b. ... sepas manejar, te daré el carro.

c. ... ella le diga que lo acompañará.

d. ... haga mucho sol en la playa.

e. ... le prometa volver temprano.

f. ... tengan que pedírmelo.

7. _____ Por mucho que...

g. ... no haya peligro de avalanchas.

8. _____ Cuando...

h. ... lo persiguiera un perro feroz.

9. _____ Escribió una explicación en caso de que...

i. ... entró el profesor.

10. _____ Ella colgó el teléfono tan pronto como...

j. ... le ha dicho que no lo quiere.

11. _____ Yo voy a llamarlos sin que...

k. ... ellos le preguntaran qué pasó.

12. _____ Los chicos estudiaron hasta que...

l. ... me hables, no te voy a escuchar.

13. _____ Una vez que...

m. ... su esposa le diera un beso.

14. _____ Su madre no le da permiso a menos que...

n. ... aprendieron la materia.

15. _____ El joven piensa esperar hasta que...

o. ... supo que era su ex novio.

Multiple choice. Select the adverbial clauses that correctly complete the sentences.

1. Los científicos dejaron de investigar el asunto antes de que _____.
   a. los políticos les den el dinero para continuar sus estudios
   b. hubieran obtenido los resultados de sus experimentos
   c. vino el presidente para felicitarlos
   d. el comité aprobó sus resultados

2. Los miembros del jurado no condenaron al criminal a pesar de que _____.
   a. el juez diga que es culpable
   b. se dice que es culpable
   c. tenían toda la evidencia necesaria
   d. tuvieran toda la evidencia necesaria

3. La señora seguía leyendo, sentada en el sofá, mientras _____.
   a. su hijo hace su tarea
   b. su hijo hacía su tarea
   c. su hijo hizo su tarea
   d. su hijo hará su tarea

4. Yo quería construir el edificio de manera que _____.
   a. no se derrumba durante el terremoto
   b. no se derrumbó durante el terremoto
   c. no se derrumbara durante un terremoto
   d. no se derrumbe durante un terremoto

5. Está nublado ahora, pero Juan y Tomás van a seguir pescando, aunque tal

   vez _____.
   a. llueva todo el día
   b. llovió ayer
   c. llovía durante la noche
   d. está lloviendo ahora

6. Maritere va a casarse con el Sr. Rubio con tal de que él _____.
   a. siempre lleve ropa de moda
   b. no deja de estudiar todos los días
   c. no dejara sus estudios de posgrado
   d. se baña de noche

7. Los González hicieron muchos sacrificios para que _____.
   a. sus hijos iban a las mejores escuelas de la ciudad
   b. sus hijos puedan triunfar en la vida
   c. sus hijos tienen los mejores juguetes
   d. sus hijos pudieran triunfar en la vida

8. Mis jefes me van a dar permiso de quedarme muy tarde en la oficina siempre

   que _____.
   a. todavía quedan otros
   b. había tiempo para hacer más
   c. lava todos los platos antes de salir
   d. escriba los informes de los equipos de investigación

9. Por favor, espérame hasta que _____.
   a. se pone el sol
   b. tu papá va a llamar pronto
   c. se vayan los otros empleados
   d. me baño en dos horas

10. Los empleados pueden salir temprano del trabajo siempre y

cuando _____.
   a. han cumplido con sus deberes
   b. terminen sus tareas del día
   c. pueden terminar el trabajo temprano
   d. habían hecho todo

EJERCICIO

5·4

Translate the following sentences from Spanish to English.

1. Era importante terminar el camino antes de que ellos comenzaran los muros.

   _____

2. La muchacha no quiso tejer el suéter a menos que su novio le comprara el estambre.

   _____

3. Había mucha gente en el parque a pesar de que llovía.

   _____

4. Arreglaron el modelo del proyecto de modo que se viera más realista.

   _____

5. Los adolescentes comían como si hubieran pasado días sin un bocado.

   _____

6. Los ladrones salieron del banco sin que nadie los viera.

   _____

7. Van a poner un anuncio en el periódico para que más gente solicite el puesto.

   _____

8. Ellos leyeron la novela de cubierta a cubierta a fin de poder discutirla.

   _____

9. Voy a salir en cuanto termine este capítulo.

_____

10. El jefe iba a escribirnos un cheque a no ser que faltaran fondos en la cuenta.

_____

Translate the following sentences from English to Spanish.

1. The team will go to bed early so that they can play better tomorrow.

_____

2. He is going to win, although he has not done well this year.

_____

3. They will study physics unless their professor recommends another class.

_____

4. Once she had climbed the mountain, she could see the ocean.

_____

5. I'll see you when you get here.

_____

6. No matter how much we practiced yesterday, we couldn't learn the game.

_____

7. Although she may write well, the editor will not hire her.

_____

8. Once you get to El Paso, crossing into Ciudad Juárez is easy.

_____

9. The children were going to play with the dog, provided their mother let them.

_____

10. He and I are going to play chess, although he usually wins.

_____

Contrary-to-fact statements

·6·

There is only one distinction you must make to master the use of the subjunctive in this, the last of the four situations in which the subjunctive is used. You must learn to recognize the difference between a cause-and-effect statement and a hypothetical one—also often called contrary-to-fact or contingency statements. Both cause-and-effect and contrary-to-fact sentences have the same basic structure—two parallel clauses, each with its particular tense. We will examine each of these in turn.

A cause-and-effect statement observes reality and makes an assertion about what will or will not happen given the current state of affairs. A cause-and-effect statement points out or indicates reality and is expressed with the indicative tenses. Thus, a cause-and-effect statement may be formed (and recognized) by the present tense in one clause to show the current situation, or *cause*, while the other clause or half of the sentence uses the future to show the *effect*, or expected result.

To exemplify a cause-and-effect sentence, let's say you are in a car with someone who drives badly. You see the person driving badly and express some logical judgment about the consequences. The cause, so to speak, is what you assert, and whether it is really true or not, it is still your take on things, so it is expressed in the present indicative tense. The effect, your judgment, is like a prophecy or prediction, and therefore is expressed in the future tense (also an indicative tense).

> Si **manejas** como loco, te **pondrán** una multa.
>
> *If you **drive** like a maniac, they **will give** you a ticket.*

Let's change this cause-and-effect statement into a hypothetical one. To put it hypothetically, if you *were not* in a car, or if your friend *were not* driving badly, but instead you were discussing what *would*, or *could*, happen to your friend if he or she *did drive* badly, you *would not use* either the present or the future, in either English or Spanish. Take a look at the following sentence. It is an example of a contrary-to-fact sentence and shows

59

which verb tenses and moods are required to construct one. So we have simply turned our cause-and-effect example above into a hypothetical, or contrary-to-fact, statement:

Si **manejaras** como loco, te **pondrían** una multa.	*If you **drove** like a maniac, they **would give** you a ticket.*

Whenever we express a speculation or conjecture about what would happen *if* certain circumstances were true at that moment, or in the past, we have no choice in either English or Spanish but to use the proper tenses and moods to do so. The main obstacle to mastering this feature of the Spanish language is, quite frankly, that many English speakers do not use the proper English tenses correctly when confronted with this situation in their own language. This is not the place to repair or point out correct English usage. However, if you do not use the tenses of English as in the examples above, you might want to consult an English college grammar text. You might find one in a used bookstore.

If English grammar is not a problem for you, then it will come as good news to learn that English and Spanish express cause-and-effect and contrary-to-fact statements in the same way, at least with regard to the tenses required in each circumstance. The only difference is that in Spanish the imperfect subjunctive is used in the *if* portion of the sentence when the hypothetical is about the present, plus the conditional in the half that expresses the consequence.

This can be seen in the preceding example, where the *imperfect subjunctive* and the *conditional* were used in tandem—the conditional shows the result, and the imperfect subjunctive sets up the hypothetical circumstance expressed by the *if* clause. Note that this contrary-to-fact sentence is expressing a conjecture about the present, despite the use of the imperfect subjunctive to do so. Note that in English, the past tense also is used in the *if* clause of a hypothetical statement, as the above example shows.

A word must be said about the *conditional* at this point. Technically, it is not a tense, but rather a mood in its own right. However, for the learner, this formal distinction is not an obstacle, because the translation of the conditional into English is always *would* plus the *base form* of the verb for the simple tense, and *would have* plus a *past participle* for the compound.

Yo **iría**.	*I **would go**.*
Ellas **habrían comido**.	*They **would have eaten**.*

Beyond this observation, the only further difficulties one might have are that (1) there are a handful of verbs that have an irregular stem, (2) the endings are all *added to the infinitive* or to the modified infinitives, and (3) the one set of endings for all verbs is exactly the same as the endings for -**er** and -**ir** verbs in the imperfect indicative (-**ía**, -**ías**, -**ía**; -**íamos**, -**íais**, -**ían**).

INFINITIVE	NEW STEM FOR FUTURE AND CONDITIONAL
decir	dir-
hacer	har-
poner	pondr-
salir	saldr-
tener	tendr-
valer	valdr-
venir	vendr-
caber	cabr-
haber	habr-
poder	podr-
querer	querr-
saber	sabr-

The verbs with irregular stems for the conditional are the same as those that have irregular stems in the future tense and they are the same stems. These are easier to remember if you notice that the stems in the second group above all end with either an **n** or an **l**. The third group can be thought of as "collapsed" infinitives, in that the theme vowel (**e, i**) of the infinitive has been dropped. That leaves only the two verbs in the first group that can simply be thought of as *really* irregular!

Returning now to the concept of hypothesis, try to recall the lists of expressions in Chapter 5. Remember how the phrase **como si** always requires the imperfect subjunctive or the pluperfect subjunctive? Now you can appreciate why—they introduce hypothetical statements.

Trabaja **como si** la vida **dependiera** de ello.   *He works **as if** his life **depended** on it.*
Se veía **como si hubiera visto** un fantasma.   *He looked **as if he had seen** a ghost.*

Next, let's shift a present hypothesis to the past. This is a common feature of Spanish and English. Returning to our example of the traveling friends, what if they had traveled together last summer? If a statement is expressed as a hypothesis about a *past* time, then the corresponding perfect, or compound, tenses are used to express this hypothetical statement about a past circumstance that *didn't happen* but *might have happened*. The *pluperfect subjunctive* is used in the *if* clause to set up the hypothetical circumstance, and the *conditional perfect* is used to show the consequence, or what *would have* happened (but never did).

The order in which the clauses are presented is unimportant. Let's examine both types of hypothetical, or contrary-to-fact, statements, one in the present, one in the past.

Si **manejaras** como loco, te **pondrían** una multa.	If you **drove** like a maniac, they **would give** you a ticket.
Te **pondrían** una multa si **manejaras** como loco.	They **would give** you a ticket if you **drove** like a maniac.
Si **hubieras manejado** como loco, te **habrían puesto** una multa.	If you **had driven** like a maniac, they **would have given** you a ticket.
Te **habrían puesto** una multa si **hubieras manejado** como loco.	They **would have given** you a ticket if you **had driven** like a maniac.

The assumption in the first example, the statement of a present hypothesis, is *not* that your traveling companion *is* driving badly, but that if he or she *were* driving badly, a ticket *would be* in order. What is fair to assert as factual is that you definitely are in a car traveling together and that your friend is driving just fine.

In the second example, the situation is simply shifted to some time in the past. Again, what is fair to assert as factual is that the two of you did take a trip together, and that your traveling companion had *not* driven badly, but if he or she *had driven* irresponsibly, a ticket *would have been* in order. Both these examples present the most common grammatical solutions possible for expressing these ideas.

You may encounter two alternatives for the imperfect subjunctive portion of this tandem construction, namely, the use of **de haber...** or **a no ser por...** followed by the conditional or compound conditional, depending on whether the hypothesis is present or past. Thus, these expressions are modified to become equivalents of the *pluperfect subjunctive* simply by the use of the infinitive of **haber** plus the past participle of **ser**.

De no haber sido por la tormenta, el avión **habría llegado** a tiempo.	**Had it not been for** the storm, the plane **would have arrived** on time.

The order in which this tandem formation is presented is not important, in either English or Spanish, but the *form used* in each half of the hypothesis is very important. It should be apparent that the sentence structure and tenses used for expressing hypotheses are very mechanical and dependable.

Memorizing two examples—one for the present, one for the past—will help you become an expert in no time. If you know the forms, including the irregular past participles (for the pluperfect subjunctive and the conditional perfect), the rest is a game of mental cut and paste.

Remember that the imperfect and pluperfect subjunctive are exclusively used in the *if* clause and the conditional and conditional perfect are used in the clause expressing the suspected result (what *would* happen or *would have* happened).

Usually, the simple forms are used in tandem and the compound ones as well, depending on whether the contrary-to-fact statement is about the present or about the past.

Logic, however, still plays a role. For instance, it is possible to say what you would do today if something had not happened last week.

<table>
<tr>
<td>Si ella fuera a almorzar conmigo esta tarde, me habría llamado la semana pasada para confirmar la cita.</td>
<td>If she were going to eat with me this afternoon, she would have called me last week to confirm the date.</td>
</tr>
</table>

In many regions of Latin America, the pluperfect subjunctive is used as an equivalent of the conditional perfect. The example above, written with the pluperfect subjunctive instead of the conditional perfect, has the same meaning (*would have*).

Si ella **fuera a almorzar** conmigo esta tarde, me **hubiera llamado** la semana pasada para confirmar la cita.

In this book, however, the conditional perfect is used for the English verb modal phrase *would have*. The advantage for English speakers is that the conditional perfect of Spanish is its exact counterpart. Therefore, if you know the handful of irregular past participles, you must only master the six forms of the conditional of the verb **haber** in order to use this important and useful compound tense.

Keep all these examples in mind, as models, as you examine the sentences in the exercises. Be on the lookout for similar situations.

EJERCICIO
6·1

Indicate whether the following English sentences are cause-and-effect (if-then) or hypothetical sentences by writing a C or an H in the blanks.

1. _____ If these sentences are easy to identify, you'll have no problems with the rest.

2. _____ If politics weren't such a dirty game, nicer people would get involved.

3. _____ Even if there were no heaven, it would be good to love one's neighbor.

4. _____ You'll be rich if you put your money on that stock.

5. _____ If only she had gone to Paris, she would have been a great model.

6. _____ Her girlfriends would play matchmaker if she weren't so sullen.

7. _____ He'll get the part in the play if he tries out.

8. _____ If you can read that bumper sticker, you're driving too close to the other car.

9. _____ He'll be convicted, if tried.

10. _____ Peace would be possible, if people weren't so stubborn.

11. _____ If he asks her to dance, she won't refuse.

12. _____ She would have turned him down if he hadn't been such a good dresser.

Using the verbs in parentheses, fill in the blanks with either the conditional, conditional perfect, imperfect subjunctive, or pluperfect subjunctive.

1. Si ellos fueran de compras, nosotros los _____. (acompañar)

2. Yo le _____ la verdad a Susana si no fuera por su malicia al oírla. (decir)

3. Si ella me _____ la verdad, le habría perdonado, tal vez. (decir)

4. Los niños dicen que _____ a la luna, pero sólo si de verdad fuera de queso. (ir)

5. Si ellos _____ los documentos, los políticos les creerían más fácilmente. (traducir)

6. Él le pediría la mano si ella _____ dejar de fumar. (poder)

7. Si nosotros _____ un sofá, ¿dónde cree Ud. que lo

   _____? (tener/poner)

8. Yo _____ que ordeñarla si tuviera una vaca. (tener)

9. Sería magnífico si mis amigos _____ la lotería. (ganar)

10. Juana dice que _____ con Tomás si se vistiera mejor. (salir)

11. Si tú pudieras hablar con el presidente, ¿qué le _____? (decir)

12. Si yo _____ lo que ella había hecho, no la habría defendido. (saber)

Translate the following sentences from Spanish to English.

1. Esos niños nunca aprenderán si siguen leyendo tiras cómicas.

   _____

2. Su padre le daría un coche a Juan si éste fuera más responsable.

   _____

3. ¿Qué pasaría si nadie quisiera ir a la guerra?

   _____

4. Si los elefantes pudieran volar, las calles del mundo estarían muy sucias.

   _____

5. Si no hay comida en casa, tendremos que ir a comprarla.

   _____

6. Si dedicaras más tiempo a tus estudios, podrías aprobar las clases.

   _____

7. Tendríamos más dinero si no lo gastáramos en tonterías.

   _____

8. Mis amigos en Tibet me llamarían si tuvieran un teléfono celular.

   _____

9. Si los políticos no derrocharan nuestro dinero, seríamos más ricos.

   _____

10. Si paso más tiempo con el subjuntivo, lo podré usar sin dificultad.

    _____

Translate the following sentences from English to Spanish.

1. What would you (**tú**) do if you had as much money as Bill Gates?

   _____

2. His friends would have come if he had told them there was a party.

   _____

3. If you have time tomorrow, we'll go to the movies.

   _____

4. We'll stay home tonight if it rains.

   _____

5. If she admitted that she lied, I would feel better.

   _____

6. I'll drive if you read the map.

   _____

7. Would you go to Mars if NASA gave you the chance?

   _____

8. I would learn to play the piano, if I had time.

   _____

9. If they had attended the conference, we would have impressed them.

   _____

10. She would convince her boss if he could understand her.

   _____

On line A, translate the following cause-and-effect, or factual or if-then, statements. Then, on line B, transform them into hypothetical statements, in Spanish. In a few cases, vocabulary hints have been given to keep you from going too far afield. Naturally, it helps to use a good dictionary.

1. If we invest in those stocks, we shall earn a lot. (**invertir en/ganar**)

   A. _____

   B. _____

2. They will sell the company if the board of directors does not oppose it. (**vender/ oponerse a**)

   A. _____

   B. _____

3. If she brings the food, we will go to the beach.

   A. _____

   B. _____

4. I will call the mechanic if the car does not run well. (**funcionar**)

   A. _____

   B. _____

5. If she wants to buy the car, her father will give her the money.

   A. _____

   B. _____

6. Even if she wants to buy the stock, he will not like it. (**gustar**)

   A. _____

   B. _____

7. If the general commands them, the troops will attack. (**mandar/atacar**)

   A. _____

   B. _____

8. It will rain if it is hot. (**hacer calor**)

    A. _____

    B. _____

9. They will die if they try to swim in the river. (**intentar** or **tratar de**)

    A. _____

    B. _____

10. If you do that again, I will complain to the manager! (**quejarse**)

    A. _____

    B. _____

11. If they bring their dog to the party, I will not let it in. (**llevar/dejar entrar**)

    A. _____

    B. _____

12. He will attend college even if his parents don't have enough money. (**asistir a**)

    A. _____

    B. _____

13. We will hire them if they do not ask for too much. (**contratar/pedir**)

    A. _____

    B. _____

14. He will return the merchandise if she has the receipt. (**devolver/comprobante**)

    A. _____

    B. _____

15. If I leave, they will not know what to do. (**irse/saber qué hacer**)

    A. _____

    B. _____

Comprehensive exercises

·7·

In all the exercises that follow, any tense or mood of the verbs may be required, both simple and compound (those formed by some conjugation of **haber** plus a past participle). Unlike the previous sections, then, any and all clause types will be found in each exercise. In the case of fill-in-the-blank formats, some blanks may require more than one word, as in the case of reflexive or compound verbs.

As you work through all the exercises, first determine what kind of clause you are faced with. Next, remember to apply the rules that govern the subjunctive usage in that type of clause to determine whether the subjunctive is necessary. Then determine which tense of the subjunctive is needed. Finally, one last reminder: be careful with regard to the agreement of verbs and subjects with respect to person and number.

In the answer keys to the multiple choice exercises in these comprehensive exercises, clause types will be identified and the rules for choosing indicative or subjunctive will be reinforced. Brief explanations about sequence of tense will also be offered since the notion of temporal logic determines which of the four tenses of the subjunctive mood must or can be used.

EJERCICIO

7·1

Fill in the blanks with the correct form of the verbs in parentheses.

1. Mi amigo vino a vivir aquí antes de que mi tía _____ con nosotros. (estar)

2. La niñera prefiere cuidar sólo a aquellos chicos que _____ vestirse a sí mismos. (saber)

3. Necesito un motor que no _____ ruido. (hacer)

4. El ayudante del cocinero cortó todo para que el cocinero

   _____ preparar la cena rápidamente. (poder)

5. Estudiamos mucho ahora a fin de _____ a casa este sábado que viene. (volver)

6. Su mamá le dijo que _____ ya que era tarde. (dormirse)

7. Si Juan no _____ pronto, vamos a tener que salir sin él. (llegar)

8. ¿No había vuelos que _____ a Tierra del Fuego en aquella época? (ir)

9. Joven, ¿qué quieres que tus padres te _____ cuando te gradúes de la universidad? (dar)

10. ¡Ah, el Sr. Gómez... claro, el nuevo candidato! Bueno, no voy a votar por él,

    aunque sí, lo _____ bien. (conocer)

11. Ella sólo quería salir con muchachos que un día le _____ la mano. (pedir)

12. Buscaban una fábrica que _____ más de una tonelada del producto por día. (producir)

13. Siempre ha sido importante _____ las deudas a tiempo. (pagar)

14. ¡Ojalá que el profesor no me _____ esto! No estoy preparado. (preguntar)

15. El dependiente de la tienda salió después de que su jefe _____ el dinero. (contar)

16. No lo dejaría volver a casa a menos que le _____ toda la historia escandalosa. (decir)

17. Tenía un caballo que _____ mal de un ojo. (mirar)

18. Tenemos un loro que _____ todo lo que oye. (repetir)

19. No hay políticos ahora que _____ a lo antiguo. (pensar)

20. Le dije al profesor que yo _____ la lección antes de venir a clase pero no me creyó. (leer)

21. Si ella lo _____ jamás habría vuelto a salir con él. ¡Qué sinvergüenza! (oír)

22. Era necesario tener secretarias que _____ muchas lenguas extranjeras. (saber)

23. Es una lástima que tú no _____ a tu amigo; le habría gustado la playa hoy. (traer)

24. Sr. Gómez, quiero que Ud. le _____ este mensaje al jefe. (dar)

25. Chicos, tan pronto como _____ los zapatos, podremos salir. (ponerse)

Matching. Select the clauses on the right that both logically and grammatically finish the sentences on the left.

1. _____ Los jugadores habían ganado...

   a. ... no tendrían miedo de nadar allí.

2. _____ Él esperaba hallar un estéreo...

   b. ... una semana laboral de 40 horas.

3. _____ Ayer perdimos el partido...

   c. ... si no fuera por la violencia constante.

4. _____ Les era una tragedia...

   d. ... si hubieran sabido que iba a llover.

5. _____ Iríamos al Medio Oriente...

   e. ... le regale una nueva caña de pescar.

6. _____ No habrían ido al parque ese día...

   f. ... no nevó ni una vez.

7. _____ Ojalá que su padre...

   g. ... que sus padres no vinieran durante la Navidad.

8. _____ Los obreros demandaban...

   h. ... porque no habíamos practicado lo suficiente.

9. _____ Era cierto que en el verano...

   i. ... antes de que el otro equipo saliera a la cancha.

10. _____ Si pudieran ver el fondo del lago...

   j. ... que reprodujera discos de 45 rpm.

Matching. Select the clauses on the right that both logically and grammatically finish the sentences begun by the independent clauses on the left.

1. _____ Vio la tienda...

    a. ... a fin de saber si era corrupto o no.

2. _____ La muchacha salía con su novio...

    b. ... con tal de que supiera quiénes iban con él.

3. _____ Ellos preferían ver películas...

    c. ... que es fácil de navegar.

4. _____ Los atletas levantaban pesas...

    d. ... en que se vendieran regalos importados.

5. _____ Buscábamos una tienda...

    e. ... en que se vendían regalos importados.

6. _____ Tenemos un velero...

    f. ... que tuvieran que ver con lo sobrenatural.

7. _____ Su papá le dio permiso de ir...

    g. ... sin que sus padres se dieran cuenta.

8. _____ Hago ejercicio...

    h. ... para ser más fuertes que sus competidores.

9. _____ Era necesario investigar al candidato...

    i. ... que le permita viajar mucho.

10. _____ Ella espera que le den un puesto...

    j. ... para adelgazar.

Multiple choice. Select the clauses that correctly complete the sentences.

1. El senador va a presentarse como candidato otra vez a menos

   que _____.
   a. no tiene suficiente dinero para una nueva campaña
   b. la prensa sabe que tiene una relación con su secretaria
   c. se revele su relación escandalosa con una secretaria
   d. sus hijos tuvieran problemas con drogas

2. Es fenomenal que _____.
   a. los Yankees van a ganar el campeonato
   b. tú ganas la lotería
   c. hace buen tiempo hoy
   d. mi amigo haya ganado la lotería

3. El entrenador les enseñaba a nadar al estilo mariposa para

   que _____.
   a. él puede recibir un trofeo por ser un buen entrenador
   b. sus padres van a estar muy impresionados
   c. pudieran competir en todos los eventos de natación
   d. ellos lo pasan bien este verano en la playa

4. Cuando llegué a casa, me frustró que _____.
   a. se me habían perdido las llaves de la casa
   b. no recibía cartas de mis amigos
   c. nadie hubiera lavado los platos
   d. no había nada que comer

5. El desfile va a seguir una ruta directa hacia el este hasta _____.
   a. la policía les dice que doblen a la derecha
   b. es hora de regresar
   c. llegar a la Casa Blanca
   d. llueve

6. El presidente nos prometió que una vez que _____.
   a. ganen la guerra, regresarán las tropas
   b. ganan la guerra, regresan las tropas
   c. ganaran la guerra, regresarían las tropas
   d. han ganado la guerra, regresarán las tropas

7. El psiquiatra le recomendó que _____.
   a. no debe ver películas violentas
   b. tome tranquilizantes
   c. debe ir de vacaciones
   d. lo visitara cada semana para psicoanalizarlo

8. Cuando eran niños, ellos siempre querían tener un perro

   que _____.
   a. duerma en casa
   b. pudiera jugar con ellos todos los días
   c. haga trucos
   d. hable como un loro

9. Hay mucho que hacer todavía pero estoy cansado. Seguiré esperando aquí hasta

   que _____.
   a. Ud. termine su tarea
   b. Ud. sigue trabajando
   c. Ud. va a seguir trabajando
   d. Ud. trabaja

10. Voy a estar dormido cuando _____.
   a. mi compañero de cuarto regrese del cine
   b. Ud. está dormido
   c. ellos vuelven del centro
   d. tú tienes que trabajar

11. Los perros corrían tras los conejos mientras _____.
   a. los cazadores esperaban la oportunidad de disparar
   b. los pájaros duermen en las ramas
   c. una ráfaga rompió el tronco de un árbol
   d. tú empezaste a desayunar

12. Los filósofos materialistas dudaban que _____.
   a. hay un mundo espiritual que no podemos tocar ni medir en esta vida
   b. Dios existía
   c. existiera tal cosa como el espíritu
   d. el ser humano tenía un espíritu

13. El capitán pirata esperaba que, cuando _____.
   a. comienza Carnaval, van a hacer fiesta
   b. la flotilla de los piratas arribara al puerto de Curaçao, la tormenta
      hubiera pasado
   c. va a pique el bergantín enemigo, nadie lo va a descubrir
   d. empieza a hacer sol, pueden limpiar sus armas

14. Fue muy emocionante que _____.
    a. la actriz muestra su gratitud a sus aficionados
    b. el director alababa a una actriz tan joven
    c. las actrices expresaran su agradecimiento tan sincero al público
    d. el actor dio dinero a un orfanato

15. No le molestó la condición de su hijo, siempre que _____.
    a. se porta bien
    b. puede jugar con otros niños
    c. pudiera hablar
    d. los otros niños lo tratan bien

16. La pareja va a ir a Cuba para su luna de miel tan pronto

    como _____.
    a. sus padres les dan los boletos de ida y vuelta
    b. ahorren suficiente dinero para hacer el viaje
    c. sacan la gorda de la lotería
    d. Fidel ya no es dictador

17. Los terroristas van a poner en libertad a los rehenes a no ser

    que _____.
    a. no les parece conveniente
    b. algún político no cumpla con lo acordado por los diplomáticos
    c. un diplomático no comete el error de defamar su religión
    d. ellos no deciden matarlos sin fórmula de justicia

18. Muy pocos cristianos de la Edad Media creían que _____.
    a. el sol se apagara todas las noches para volver a encenderse por
       la mañana
    b. las estrellas fueran linternas llevadas por ángeles o espíritus
    c. el mundo fuera llano
    d. el mundo era redondo como una naranja

19. Los alpinistas suizos subieron la montaña Everest como

    si _____.
    a. hubieran nacido sólo para ello
    b. era la cosa más natural del mundo
    c. fue una colina cualquiera
    d. habían nacido para hacerlo

20. El autor de este libro se alegra de que _____.
   a. has comprado su libro y te desea lo mejor
   b. hayas comprado su libro y espera que te sea útil
   c. estás aprendiendo la lengua de Cervantes
   d. no encuentra difícil el subjuntivo

Translate the following sentences from Spanish to English.

1. Los novios se casaron antes de besarse ante el altar.

   _____

2. Esperas que yo no espere que me esperes.

   _____

3. Te buscaba por todas partes, esperando que me echaras de menos.

   _____

4. Los pescadores lanzaron sus barcos de vela al mar a pesar de la lluvia.

   _____

5. Si todas las suegras se murieran, los esposos valdrían más.

   _____

6. Los chicos esperaban que San Nicolás les trajera muchos juguetes.

   _____

7. El joven la va a sacar a bailar tan pronto como la vea.

   _____

8. Él vino a EE.UU. esperando tener mejor fortuna.

   _____

9. El platillo volador desapareció tan pronto como había aparecido.

   _____

10. Decidí que iba a jugar a los billares con Juan cuando viniera al bar.

    _____

11. No había ningún libro en la librería que tratara el asunto que me interesaba.

    _____

12. —¿Vas de compras?
    —Sí, a pesar de que mis papás no me hayan dado mucho dinero.

    _____

13. Los políticos querían dárselo todo a contratistas corruptos.

    _____

14. ¿Prefieres música que tenga buena letra a la que sea bailable?

    _____

15. Después de salir de casa no es el momento de preguntarte si has apagado
    el horno.

    _____

16. Creen que van a Acapulco, con tal de que haya un vuelo económico este fin
    de semana.

    _____

17. ¿Quieres acompañarla a la cafetería o prefieres que ella vaya sola?

    _____

18. Necesitamos una persona que sepa Swahili y que sea capaz de enseñarlo.

    _____

19. Juana quería una sortija que fuera más elegante y esperaba que Juan se
    la comprara.

    _____

20. Ese adolescente sólo quiere una novia que haga lo que a él le interesa.

    _____

Translate the following sentences from English to Spanish. In a few cases, vocabulary hints have been given.

1. It was a pity that her husband had abandoned her with all those children.

_____

2. The pilots were hoping the flight attendants would serve dinner.

_____

3. The little girl won't eat the bears' soup unless she is very hungry.

_____

4. His teachers always told him to apply himself to his studies. (**meterse de lleno en**)

_____

5. When they went diving, they were afraid of what they might see. (**bucear**)

_____

6. If she went to the party, then he saw her; but I doubt that she went.

_____

7. If she is rejected one more time, I think she will cry.

_____

8. When he heard the news, he doubted they had told him the truth.

_____

9. The bears were angry because the little girl had eaten their soup.

_____

10. There wasn't anyone who felt sad when Susan died.

_____

11. If you were to go to Cuba, what places would you visit?

_____

12. After the animals ate, they fell asleep.

_____

13. They hoped he would arrive before it got dark. (**anochecer**)

_____

14. Before she learned to drive, she never wanted to do anything.

_____

15. Once you have finished this book, you will be able to use the subjunctive correctly.

_____

16. Do you think there would be anyone who would care if they had bad luck?

_____

17. If you could sell it to us for less, we would order more. (**pedir**)

_____

18. If you want peace, it is necessary that you fight for justice.

_____

19. If it had not been for your parents, you would not be here.

_____

20. Don't forget to close the door after you enter or exit the building.

_____

Select the appropriate verbs from the list below and fill in the blanks with the proper tense and mood. Some verbs may be used more than once. Some blanks may require compound tenses.

asistir	decidir	nacer	seguir	vivir
casarse	graduarse	pagar	ser	
conocerse	gustar	poder	tener	
criarse	llevar	querer	terminar	

Antes de que mis padres (1) _____, ellos (2) _____ en

pueblos muy diferentes y tenían ideas muy distintas sobre la vida. Como mi papá era

de una familia granjera, cuando ellos (3) _____ él esperaba que a ella le

(4) _____ vivir en el campo. Ella, al contrario, aunque (5) _____

en las montañas, no (6) _____ aceptar la idea. Ella prefería que ellos

(7) _____ una vida más urbana que campestre, que (8) _____

electrodomésticos que siempre (9) _____ los más modernos posibles y

que, en caso de que (10) _____ hijos, que éstos (11) _____

a escuelas privadas y exclusivas.

Bueno, cuando yo (12) _____, ellos (13) _____

mudarse a otro estado donde mi mamá prefería que mi papá (14) _____

sus estudios. Claro, los dos tenían la esperanza de que cuando él (15) _____

sus estudios de posgrado, (16) _____ ganar más dinero. Así

(17) _____ en efecto, porque cuando (18) _____, él obtuvo

un puesto que le (19) _____ el doble de lo que habría ganado si no se

(20) _____.

*Select the appropriate verbs from the list below and fill in the blanks with the
proper tense and mood. Some verbs may be used more than once. Some blanks
may require compound tenses.*

acordarse	hacer	preparar	tener
dejar	limpiar	prestar	usar
empezar	manejar	sacar	
estar	pedir	ser	

Los padres de Tomás no creían que él (1) _____ lo suficientemente

responsable como para usar el coche de la familia. A pesar de que él (2) _____

buenas notas en la escuela, era obvio por la manera distraída en que hacía casi todo

que si (3) _____ un coche solo, (4) _____ un accidente

automobilístico. Aunque Tomás casi siempre (5) _____ lo que sus padres

le pedían que (6) _____, no (7) _____ de los detalles y se

quejaba de que le (8) _____ que (9) _____ "tanto", según

decía él. Esto es lo que a sus padres les causaba preocupación. Decidieron que a

menos que él (10) _____ más atención a todo, no le iban a permitir que

(11) _____ el coche.

Un día, cuando sus padres regresaron del trabajo, les sorprendió que Tomás ya

(12) _____ la cena para toda la familia y que la mesa (13) _____

puesta. Se lo agradecieron, pero no le prometieron nada, ya que querían saber si sólo

había sido un capricho o si de veras estaba madurando. Durante varias semanas, al

llegar a casa, les asombraba que incluso (14) _____ el garaje ya, y que su

recámara (15) _____ limpia. Por fin creyeron que era probable que

Tomás (16) _____ a responsabilizarse más y le aseguraron que, con tal

de que no (17) _____ de portarse como adulto, hasta le comprarían su

propio carro. Entonces, le preguntaron qué tipo de carro quería.

Les dio las gracias, y luego con mucha calma les dijo que "por favor" le buscaran

un coche que (18) _____ aire acondicionado y un reproductor de CD.

Esto les pareció razonable. Luego, que prefería que (19) _____ rojo

también. Ellos le dijeron que esto era muy factible. Y luego que, además, "si no era

demasiado pedir", que (20) _____ un Mercedes 450 SE. Al escuchar esto,

sus padres casi perdieron la paciencia y se preguntaban por qué le habían hecho tal

promesa tan pronto.

Select the appropriate verbs from the list below and fill in the blanks with the proper tense and mood. Some verbs may be used more than once. Some blanks may require compound tenses.

congelarse	hacer	ocurrir	recomendar	venir
costar	incluir	pagar	revelar	
encontrar	ir	pedir	ser	
estar	medir	querer	tener	

Mi hermano quiere comprar una computadora nueva pero no sabe precisamente

cuáles (1) _____ los rasgos que más le deben importar. Dice que lo que

quiere es una computadora que (2) _____ todas las herramientas que

necesita para su pasatiempo favorito, los videojuegos. Así que creo que va a buscar

una marca que (3) _____ tarjetas de video y sonido. Además, según él,

necesita una que (4) _____ una ordenadora de palabras y mucha

memoria. Lo más importante, es que el teclado no (5) _____ y que

(6) _____ con un teclado y un ratón de mando a distancia. En cuanto a

la pantalla, dice que busca una que (7) _____ por lo menos 17 pulgadas.

Él tiene una computadora ahora que (8) _____ a cada rato y esto lo

vuelve loco porque siempre (9) _____ en medio de un proyecto

importante o en un momento emocionante de uno de sus videojuegos.

En cuanto al precio, ahí está el problema. Necesita que (10) _____

menos de $1.500 pero con todo lo que desea en cuanto a herramientas y periféricos,

dudo que (11) _____ una por menos de $2.000. Además, nuestros

padres le dijeron que no (12) _____ con tarjeta de crédito, sino en efectivo. Ya que no tiene tanto en su cuenta, temo que me (13) _____ a

pedir un préstamo sin intereses, como favor, y que me (14) _____ que

no se lo (15) _____ a nuestros padres. Aunque es mi hermano y lo

(16) _____ mucho, no sé qué debo hacer. Si tú (17) _____

en mi lugar, ¿qué (18) _____? ¿Qué me (19) _____ que

(20) _____?

EJERCICIO
7·10

Select the appropriate verbs from the list below and fill in the blanks with the proper tense and mood. Some verbs may be used more than once, some not at all. Some blanks may require compound tenses.

buscar	decir	indicar	recetar	tomar
captivar	enseñar	leer	saber	ver
comer	escuchar	llenar	ser	visitar
dar	hacer	poder	tener	

Cuando don Eugenio quería que las enfermeras le (1) _____ de alta en el

hospital, ellas le (2) _____ que (3) _____ unos formularios y

que (4) _____ con cuidado las instrucciones que tenía que seguir en

cuanto a cómo y cuándo tomar los medicamentos que su médico le (5) _____

el día anterior.

No le molestaba nada a don Eugenio que le (6) _____ que dar esas

instrucciones. Lo que sí le pesaba era que el médico le (7) _____ que su condición le obligaría a seguir tomando ciertos medicamentos para siempre. Aunque

su condición no (8) _____ nada grave, le hacía la vida un poco difícil

porque su esposa siempre le tenía que decir que (9) _____ esa píldora a

esa hora. Le parecía que su vida no consistía en otra cosa que en tomar medicinas.

Lo que le agradaba más y le hacía la vida un deleite era que dos veces por

semana le (10) _____ sus dos nietas, unas chiquillas de 3 y 5 años, que

(11) _____ hijas de su hijo mayor, Carlos. Siempre le pedían que les

(12) _____ un libro de cuentos de hadas. Su hijo le había dicho que

prefería que (13) _____ algo más útil, pero don Eugenio sabía contar los

cuentos de manera que (14) _____ su atención.

Un día, para agradar a su hijo, después de que todos (15) _____,

don Eugenio decidió que era importante que ellas (16) _____ un

programa educativo en la tele. Por ser un buen padre, Carlos quería saber algo sobre

el contenido antes de que las pequeñas (17) _____ verlo. Cuando él

(18) _____ que iba a tratar de la vida de una familia de osos, les

(19) _____ su permiso y esperaba que su padre, el abuelo,

(20) _____ más programas sobre animales en la naturaleza.

Select the appropriate verbs from the list below and fill in the blanks with the proper tense and mood. Some verbs may be used more than once. Some blanks may require compound tenses.

construir	funcionar	inventar	ser
contar	gustar	poder	servir
depender	haber	preguntar	tener
existir	hacer	resolver	votar

¿Te (1) _____ alguna vez cómo (2) _____ el mundo si el

automóvil jamás (3) _____ ? ¡Cuánto más espacio (4) _____

para parques, casas, granjas, para grandes extensiones de tierra que podrían dejarse

en su estado virgen! Pero, me preguntas, si no (5) _____ coches, pues,

¿cómo (6) _____ la gente ir al trabajo o, lo que es más, viajar largas

distancias en poco tiempo? Es cierto que (7) _____ que haber grandes

sistemas de transporte público, pero la pregunta es, ¿cómo coordinarlos?

Si tú (8) _____ volver a inventar algo para el transporte, tanto para

el ciudadano particular como para la ciudadanía como colectividad, ¿qué tipo de

sistema o sistemas (9) _____ tú? Por mi parte, me (10) _____

que el sistema no (11) _____ de combustibles fósiles, sino que

(12) _____ un sistema que (13) _____ con el

uso de energía eléctrica. Esto (14) _____ bien al público con tal de que

se (15) _____ suficientes fábricas para producir la potencia eléctrica

necesaria para cargar o recargar los motores. Si todos los motores (16) _____ con pilas, o baterías, solares más eficientes que las que (17) _____ ahora,

ni habría necesidad de construir tantas fábricas para generar la potencia eléctrica. La

situación del mundo actual es tal que a menos que nosotros

(18) _____ algo, y pronto, la contaminación producida por los

hidrocarburos va a destruir los ecosistemas a nivel mundial. Para que la situación se

(19) _____, los políticos tendrán que escuchar a los científicos y al

pueblo cuando (20) _____ a favor de sistemas eficientes.

EJERCICIO

7·12

*Select the appropriate verbs from the list below and fill in the blanks with the
proper tense and mood. Some verbs may be used more than once. Some blanks
may require compound tenses.*

aplicar	guardar	pasar	tener
congratularse	imaginarse	ser	tratar
criarse	llevar	soler	valer
emplear	nacer	suceder	

Siempre (1) _____ posible decir que si las circunstancias o eventos de la

juventud no (2) _____ como (3) _____, la vida que uno

(4) _____ ahora (5) _____ muy distinta de lo que

(6) _____. Es curioso que todos, los de buena y mala fortuna,

(7) _____ esta fórmula, éstos para no (8) _____ que

aceptar la responsabilidad de sus infortunios, y aquéllos para (9) _____

por las decisiones tomadas.

Se (10) _____ pensar así cuando se (11) _____ de

cuestiones de amor, salud o dinero, pero (12) _____ un momento qué

(13) _____ si se (14) _____ a las actitudes que uno

(15) _____ acerca de la política o de cuestiones de raza o de religión.

Pues, los que (16) _____ en ambientes racistas (17) _____

racistas; un rico, si (18) _____ pobre tal vez (19) _____

opiniones distintas sobre cómo resolver la pobreza. ¿No cree Ud. que

(20) _____ la pena pensar en estos temas de vez en cuando para

reorientar sus valores hacia el mundo y los demás?

EJERCICIO

7·13

Select the appropriate verbs from the list below and fill in the blanks with the proper tense and mood. Some verbs may be used more than once. Some blanks may require compound tenses.

alegrarse	cumplir	gustar	ir
buscar	decidir	haber	poder
casarse	decir	hablar	salir
conocer	encantar	interesar	ser

Mi hermana Laura (1) _____ soltera hasta que (2) _____

treinta años. Siempre (3) _____ que (4) _____ con tal de

que (5) _____ encontrar a un hombre guapo y rico; por supuesto, a

menos que no le (6) _____ viajar. Aunque (7) _____ con

varios hombres con posibilidades, después de no tener suerte con ninguno,

(8) _____ quedarse soltera. Cuando oí esto, le dije que iba a ayudarle

para que yo (9) _____ tío un día de éstos. Mientras tanto, ella

(10) _____ un trabajo en que (11) _____ más hombres que

mujeres. Claro, todavía buscaba un novio a quien le (12) _____ los

lugares exóticos, y deseaba que a éste le (13) _____ viajar. Luego, quería

además que (14) _____ varias lenguas, pero dudaba que ella

(15) _____ encontrar a un hombre con todas estas características.

Era cierto que allí, por lo menos, no había ninguno que (16) _____ tan

interesante. Pero se sorprendió mucho cuando (17) _____ a Miguel.

Ahora está muy contenta y (18) _____ de que tan pronto como

(19) _____ ellos (20) _____ a viajar a Europa.

Select the appropriate verbs from the list below and fill in the blanks with the proper tense and mood. Some verbs may be used more than once. Some blanks may require compound tenses.

brillar	graduarme	obtener	permitir	ser
depender	gustar	pagar	poder	tener
escuchar	hacer	pasar	quedarse	vivir
estudiar	ir	pensar	seguir	

Mis hermanos no quieren que yo (1) _____ en casa cuando ven que

(2) _____ buen tiempo y que el sol (3) _____ . Es

maravilloso que nosotros (4) _____ cerca de la playa y que

(5) _____ ir a la playa cuando nos (6) _____ para hacer

surfing o simplemente para tomar el sol. A veces, les molesta a nuestros padres que

(7) _____ tanto tiempo allí. Ellos prefieren que (8) _____

porque dicen que no quieren que (9) _____ que pasar la vida haciendo

trabajos que (10) _____ poco. Cuando yo (11) _____ de la

universidad el año que viene, me han dicho que esperan que yo (12) _____

mis estudios y que (13) _____ a una escuela de posgraduados

prestigiosa. No se lo he dicho todavía, pero me molesta que ellos siempre

(14) _____ en el dinero y en cosas materiales. Por supuesto, si yo

(15) _____ un buen trabajo después que me (16) _____

tener muchos lujos en la vida, esto (17) _____ fantástico, pero no voy a

preocuparme tanto por eso. Mi hermana mayor no está de acuerdo conmigo. Ella

siempre me dice que les (18) _____ porque no quiere que yo

(19) _____ de ella en el futuro. Lo que más me molesta es que ella

(20) _____ razón.

Multiple choice. Select the clauses that correctly complete the sentences.

1. Juanita se alegró de que _____.
   a. el vuelo llegó a tiempo
   b. el vuelo llegaba a tiempo
   c. el vuelo hubiera llegado a tiempo
   d. el vuelo llega a tiempo

2. Cuando llegamos al aeropuerto, supimos que _____.
   a. el garaje estaba lleno y no había lugar para estacionar
   b. el garaje está lleno y no hay lugar para estacionar
   c. el garaje estará lleno y no habrá lugar para estacionar
   d. el garaje se haya llenado y no haya lugar para estacionar

3. Cuando vayas al extranjero, es importante _____.
   a. que tienes un pasaporte
   b. que tengas un pasaporte
   c. tener un pasaporte
   d. *b* and *c*

4. Ernesto, por favor, haznos saber tan pronto como _____.
   a. has facturado el equipaje
   b. hayas facturado el equipaje
   c. habías facturado el equipaje
   d. hubieras facturado el equipaje

5. Siempre me molesta cuando _____.
   a. hay mucha confusión en la sala de recogida de equipaje
   b. haya mucha confusión en la sala de recogida de equipaje
   c. hubiera mucha confusión en la sala de recogida de equipaje
   d. habría mucha confusión en la sala de recogida de equipaje

6. A mi mamá no le gusta que _____.
   a. hacemos cola por una hora
   b. hagamos cola por una hora
   c. hicimos cola por una hora
   d. hacíamos cola por una hora

7. Habríamos llegado más temprano al hotel _____.
   a. si no hubiéramos tenido que pasar por la aduana
   b. si no vamos a pasar por la aduana
   c. si no habíamos pasado por la aduana
   d. si no pasamos por la aduana

8. Llevaban fruta en sus maletas, así que tenían miedo de que los inspectores
   agrícolas _____.
   a. se la quitaban
   b. se la quitan
   c. se la quiten
   d. se la quitaran

9. Los pasajeros se alegran de que _____.
   a. no se permitan armas de fuego a bordo
   b. no se permiten armas de fuego a bordo
   c. no se permitirían armas de fuego a bordo
   d. no se permitirán armas de fuego a bordo

10. Yo prefiero que _____.
   a. me reservan un asiento junto a la ventana y no en el pasillo
   b. me reservarán un asiento junto a la ventana y no en el pasillo
   c. me reserven un asiento junto a la ventana y no en el pasillo
   d. me reservarían un asiento junto a la ventana y no en el pasillo

11. Veo que _____.
   a. tú compres un boleto para la clase económica
   b. tú hubieras comprado un boleto para la clase económica
   c. tú hayas comprado un boleto para la clase económica
   d. tú compraste un boleto para la clase económica

12. El agente de viajes no cree que _____.
   a. ningún vuelo hace escala en Kingston, procedente de Mérida, con destino a la Habana
   b. ningún vuelo haga escala en Kingston, procedente de Mérida, con destino a la Habana
   c. ningún vuelo hizo escala en Kingston, procedente de Mérida, con destino a la Habana
   d. ningún vuelo hacía escala en Kingston, procedente de Mérida, con destino a la Habana

13. Quiero encontrar una aerolínea que _____.
   a. me permita usar el teléfono móvil durante el vuelo
   b. me permite usar el teléfono móvil durante el vuelo
   c. me permitiría usar el teléfono móvil durante el vuelo
   d. me permitió usar el teléfono móvil durante el vuelo

14. Los reglamentos no permiten que _____.
   a. los pasajeros consumen bebidas compradas en la tienda libre de impuestos
   b. los pasajeros consuman bebidas compradas en la tienda libre de impuestos
   c. los pasajeros consumieran bebidas compradas en la tienda libre de impuestos
   d. los pasajeros consumían bebidas compradas en la tienda libre de impuestos

15. Juan abrochó el cinturón de seguridad antes de que _____.
   a. el avión despegara
   b. el avión despegue
   c. el avión haya despegado
   d. el avión hubiera despegado

16. Vamos a almorzar en el aeropuerto después de que _____.
    a. el avión ha aterrizado
    b. el avión aterriza
    c. el avión aterrizara
    d. el avión aterrice

17. Esperamos tener un asistente de vuelo que _____.
    a. sepa hablar español
    b. sabe hablar español
    c. sabía hablar español
    d. sabrá hablar español

18. Aunque a Juan no le gustó, la situación no tenía remedio, y él _____.
    a. tenga que leer en la sala de embarque a causa de la demora
    b. tuvo que leer en la sala de embarque a causa de la demora
    c. tendría que leer en la sala de embarque a causa de la demora
    d. tuviera que leer en la sala de embarque a causa de la demora

19. Les gustó a los niños cuando la asistente de vuelo les dijo que _____.
    a. abordaran el avión
    b. abordaron el avión
    c. abordaban el avión
    d. abordarán el avión

20. Señor, es urgente que _____.
    a. Ud. seguirá las instrucciones de los asistentes de vuelo
    b. Ud. sigue las instrucciones de los asistentes de vuelo
    c. Ud. siga las instrucciones de los asistentes de vuelo
    d. Ud. siguió las instrucciones de los asistentes de vuelo

EJERCICIO
7·16

Matching. Select the clauses on the right that both logically and grammatically finish the sentences begun by the independent clauses on the left.

1. _____ El mesero me recomendó...

   a. ... antes de que llegaran los meseros.

2. _____ Las niñas querían...

   b. ... un sándwich cubano que fuera auténtico.

3. _____ Le dije a la mesera...

   c. ... que se usa para hacer pozole.

4. _____ Los cocineros estaban en la cocina...

d. ... que yo pidiera los tacos al carbón.

5. _____ Fui a Miami porque buscaba...

e. ... que sus mamás les enseñaran a hacer chilaquiles

6. _____ María siempre pide...

f. ... el arroz con pollo que se prepara en casa.

7. _____ Su abuela necesitaba el maíz...

g. ... que yo quería mi bistec a término medio.

8. _____ Mi novia y yo les pedimos...

h. ... huevos fritos con tal de que estén bien cocidos

9. _____ A ella le gusta...

i. ... tan pronto como se sirvió el arroz con pollo

10. _____ Los invitados se sentaron a la mesa...

j. ... que nos hicieran dos cafés con leche.

EJERCICIO
7·17

Multiple choice. Select the clauses that correctly complete the sentences.

1. Los huéspedes en ese hotel querían cuartos que _____.
   a. incluyan el desayuno
   b. incluían el desayuno
   c. incluyeron el desayuno
   d. incluyeran el desayuno

2. Se prohíbe que _____.
   a. los menores de edad entran en el bar
   b. los menores de edad entren en el bar
   c. los menores de edad entrarán en el bar
   d. los menores de edad entrarían en el bar

3. Yo me quejé de que _____.
   a. el servicio a los cuartos fue lento
   b. el servicio a los cuartos hubiera sido lento
   c. el servicio a los cuartos fuera lento
   d. el servicio a los cuartos era lento

4. La gerencia sospechaba que _____.
   a. los descuentos ofrecidos en su sitio web resultarán en más reservaciones
   b. los descuentos ofrecidos en su sitio web hayan resultado en más reservaciones
   c. los descuentos ofrecidos en su sitio web resultaran en más reservaciones
   d. los descuentos ofrecidos en su sitio web resulten en más reservaciones

5. Creemos que la temporada turística este año resultará en ganancias que _____.
   a. vayan a ser mayores con respecto al mismo período del año pasado
   b. van a ser mayores con respecto al mismo período del año pasado
   c. hayan sido mayores con respecto al mismo período del año pasado
   d. son mayores con respecto al mismo período del año pasado

6. ¿Desea Ud. un cuarto que _____?
   a. tuviera una vista del mar o de las montañas
   b. tenía una vista del mar o de las montañas
   c. tendrá una vista del mar o de las montañas
   d. tenga una vista del mar o de las montañas

7. Los salvavidas regañaron a los niños que se metieron en la piscina antes de que _____.
   a. la abrieron
   b. la abrieran
   c. la abran
   d. la abrían

8. Se va a construir un bar en medio de la piscina para que _____.
   a. los turistas pueden nadar y tomar cocteles
   b. los turistas podían nadar y tomar cocteles
   c. los turistas puedan nadar y tomar cocteles
   d. los turistas pudieran nadar y tomar cocteles

9. Vamos a tener *wifi* después de que _____.
   a. la compañía decida cuál proveedor de servicios prefiere
   b. la compañía decide cuál proveedor de servicios prefiere
   c. la compañía decidió cuál proveedor de servicios prefiere
   d. la compañía decidiera cuál proveedor de servicios prefiere

10. Habría más diversiones en el hotel para niños pequeños _____.
    a. si hay más espacio para construir un jardín de recreo infantil
    b. si había más espacio para construir un jardín de recreo infantil
    c. si hubo más espacio para construir un jardín de recreo infantil
    d. si hubiera más espacio para construir un jardín de recreo infantil

11. Tenemos una lavandería y tintorería en caso de que _____.
    a. Ud. quiere o necesita que se lave la ropa
    b. Ud. quiera o necesite que se lave la ropa
    c. Ud. va a querer o necesitar que se lave la ropa
    d. Ud. quería o necesitaba que se lavara la ropa

12. Verá qué linda vista tiene cuando _____.
    a. Ud. subió a su cuarto
    b. Ud. sube a su cuarto
    c. Ud. suba a su cuarto
    d. Ud. subiera a su cuarto

13. Me gustó mucho mi tiempo en el hotel aunque _____.
    a. no hay agua caliente
    b. no hubo agua caliente
    c. no hubiera agua caliente
    d. no habrá agua caliente

14. Hicimos una reservación hace semanas para que _____.
    a. no tuviéramos que esperar tanto tiempo en el lobby
    b. no tengamos que esperar tanto tiempo en el lobby
    c. no teníamos que esperar tanto tiempo en el lobby
    d. no tendríamos que esperar tanto tiempo en el lobby

15. ¿No tendrán un cuarto que _____?
    a. costó menos
    b. cuesta menos
    c. cueste menos
    d. costaba menos

16. Les recomendamos que _____.
    a. no dejan dinero en su cuarto
    b. no dejarán dinero en su cuarto
    c. no dejarían dinero en su cuarto
    d. no dejen dinero en su cuarto

17. Ofrecemos excursiones en barco para los que _____.
    a. quisieron pescar
    b. quieran pescar
    c. quieren pescar
    d. querían pescar

18. Háganos saber cuando _____.
    a. están listos para ir al aeropuerto
    b. estén listos para ir al aeropuerto
    c. estaban listos para ir al aeropuerto
    d. estuvieran listos para ir al aeropuerto

19. El botones no nos permitió que _____.
    a. llevemos las maletas
    b. llevamos las maletas
    c. llevábamos las maletas
    d. lleváramos las maletas

20. Antes de nadar, era importante que _____.
    a. ellos leyeran las reglas
    b. ellos lean las reglas
    c. ellos leían las reglas
    d. ellos leerían las reglas

Select the appropriate verbs from the list below and fill in the blanks with the proper tense and mood. Some verbs may be used more than once. Some blanks may require compound tenses.

almorzar	ayudar	buscar
cerrar	decir	encontrar
empezar	escribir	gustar
ir	llegar	necesitar
pedir	poder	quedar
quitar	regresar	saber
ser	tener	

María me dijo, mientras (1) _____ con mi amigo Alberto, que ella tenía

que comprarse una nueva falda y unas blusas, antes de que se (2) _____

las tiendas en el centro comercial. El próximo viernes, volaría a San Francisco, así que

era urgente que nosotros (3) _____ lo antes posible. En caso de que una

tienda no (4) _____ lo que ella (5) _____, tendríamos

tiempo para que (6) _____ a otra. Se preocupaba de que la selección

(7) _____ limitada o de que algo no le (8) _____ bien.

También me dijo que quería que yo le (9) _____ a buscar accesorios para

el conjunto. Salimos del restaurante para ir en mi carro y le dije que cuando

(10) _____ a mi carro, ella nos (11) _____ una lista de los

ingredientes que yo (12) _____ para que nosotros (13) _____

preparar la receta que yo (14) _____ en línea. Ella sabe que yo

(15) _____ cocinar bien y esperaba que cuando (16) _____

a casa, ella (17) _____ descansar un rato mientras yo (18) _____

a preparar la cena. Muchos no me creen cuando les (19) _____ que, para

mí, cocinar me (20) _____ el estrés; les parece imposible que eso

(21) _____ posible. Aunque sí, me gustó mucho cocinar esa noche, no

me (22) _____ ayudarle a buscar accesorios para su nuevo conjunto,

porque siempre me inquieta que una mujer me (23) _____ mis consejos

sobre la moda.

EJERCICIO
7·19

Fill in the blanks with the correct form of the verbs in parentheses.

1. Busco una inversión que _____ un mínimo del siete por ciento al
   año. (rendir)

2. Mi tío tenía una cartera de inversiones que _____ dos millones de
   dólares. (valer)

3. Se espera que el Producto Interno Bruto Nacional _____ el del año
   pasado. (exceder)

4. No le importaba a él que la bolsa _____ de tendencia alcista o bajista: siempre invertía. (ser)

5. Si _____ cincuenta dólares más cada mes, ¿en que los gastarías? (tener)

6. Es muy recomendable que se les _____ a los niños a ahorrar. (enseñar)

7. Es lamentable que muchos _____ sus casas en 2008. (perder)

8. Los inquilinos se quejaban de que el costo de la vivienda _____. (subir)

9. No había ninguna acción en su cartera cuyo valor _____ aumentado antes de la crisis. (haber)

10. Mi asesor me recomienda que _____ las acciones que tengo en esa compañía. (vender)

11. Hay que salir del mercado antes de que _____. (quebrar)

12. Creo que he encontrado una compañía que _____ una buena inversión. (ser)

13. Después de que _____ esta casa, su primo construyó otra, para venderla. (comprar)

14. Si _____ en efectivo, no tendría que pedir un préstamo. (pagar)

15. Te aconsejo que _____ la deuda estudiantil lo antes posible. (saldar)

16. Ella desea un ascenso que _____ un aumento de sueldo. (incluir)

17. Si yo _____ fiarme de ellos, seguiría sus consejos. (poder)

18. Ojalá que mi abogado _____ disponible ahora hacerle una consulta. (estar)

19. Hay que seguir invirtiendo mientras no _____ indicaciones de una tendencia bajista. (haber)

20. Juan habría ganado mucho en la bolsa si _____ invertido a tiempo. (haber)

Fill in the blanks with the correct form of the verbs in parentheses.

1. Debes cambiar la dieta para que no _____ un infarto. (sufrir)

2. A menos que _____ de fumar, vas a tener problemas pulmonares. (dejar)

3. Es posible que, por razones genéticas, algunos no _____ bajar de peso tan fácilmente. (poder)

4. Si mi tía no _____ fumado, no habría sufrido de hipertensión. (haber)

5. El café hace que el ritmo cardíaco se _____. (acelerar)

6. Fue necesario que el médico le _____ imágenes por resonancia magnética. (sacar)

7. Es cierto que todos nosotros _____ a morir algún día. (ir)

8. Es cierto que algunos remedios caseros _____ efecto. (surtir)

9. No hay niño que no _____ miedo de las inyecciones. (tener)

10. El médico le permitió a mi papá que _____ cuatro onzas de carne al día. (comer)

11. Muchos se sorprenden que Fidel _____ de fumar en 1985. (dejar)

12. Me alegro de que mi hija ahora se _____ mejor. (alimentar)

13. Después de una cirugía, es importante que se _____ para caminar lo antes posible. (levantar)

14. La familia Cardona se alegró de que el médico le _____ de alta a su mamá. (dar)

15. Me importaba mucho que mis hijas _____ al médico cada año cuando eran pequeñas. (ver)

16. Es una vergüenza que todavía no _____ seguro médico universal en este país. (haber)

17. Me chocó que un médico _____ que una presión arterial de 170/100 era normal. (decir)

18. Se requiere que los pacientes _____ el formulario de consentimiento informado. (firmar)

19. Dile al niño que se _____ la pastilla para la tos dos veces al día, y con comida. (tomar)

20. Les va a seguir preocupando a los vivos que los precios funerarios

_____ subiendo. (seguir)

Select the appropriate verbs from the list below and fill in the blanks with the proper tense and mood. Some verbs may be used more than once. Some blanks may require compound tenses.

aparecer	aprender	enseñar
equivocar	estar	explotar
hacer	indicar	inventar
invitar	ir	obligar
perder	prender	querer
quemar	romper	saber
salir	ser	tener

Antes de que yo (1) _____ a usar un procesador de textos, apenas

(2) _____ escribir a máquina. Cuando mi amigo Carlos me

(3) _____ al laboratorio de informática, yo no (4) _____

cómo mi vida (5) _____ a cambiar para siempre. Tenía miedo de que yo

(6) _____ la computadora si me (7) _____ de botón. Hasta

temía que se (8) _____ o se (9) _____; pero una vez que él

me (10) _____ los pasos e instrucciones muy precisas que había de

seguir, para que yo (11) _____ la computadora e (12) _____

mis proyectos y luego (13) _____ sin problema, entonces, yo

(14) _____ la confianza para seguir aprendiendo. Él me (15) _____

a usar el teclado numérico para escribir los acentos en español y cómo crear carpetas

y guardar mis documentos en un disquete. Hoy en día, se realiza esto en una

"memoria USB" o "llave Maya". Me encantaba que mi trabajo no se (16) _____

al apagar la computadora y que al volver a prenderla y enchufar el disquete, mi

trabajo (17) _____ allí otra vez, ante mis ojos, como en la noche anterior.

Me fascinaba que, al teclear, las letras luminosas se me (18) _____ sobre

el fondo oscuro de la pantalla. Aunque (19) _____ mucho desde

entonces, todavía (20) _____ que todo (21) _____ tan

sencillo como antes de que se (22) _____ las computadoras. Prefiero

métodos de composición que no me (23) _____ a ser ingeniero.

EJERCICIO
7·22

Matching. Select the clauses on the right that both logically and grammatically finish the sentences begun by the independent clauses on the left.

1. _____ Mi hermano tenía una grabación...

2. _____ Yo iría al teatro...

3. _____ No te voy a creer...

4. _____ Juana me dijo que me acompañaría...

5. _____ Este chico estudia mucho...

6. _____ Su mamá les dijo que iban al zoológico...

a. ... sin que yo me diera cuenta.

b. que nos guste a todos.

c. para que lo acepten en la universidad.

d. si no costaran tanto los boletos.

e. ... con tal de que mis amigos no fumaran.

f. ... aunque tenía dinero.

7. _____ Estamos buscando una película...

8. _____ Mi hermana nunca me prestaba un peso...

9. _____ Mi novia cambió el canal en la tele...

10. _____ Yo voy a lavar la ropa...

g. ... aunque me lo repitas cien veces.

h. ... que había hecho en un concierto en vivo.

i. ... tan pronto como se pusieran los zapatos.

j. ...después de que tú salgas para la escuela.

EJERCICIO
7·23

Select the appropriate verbs from the list below and fill in the blanks with the proper tense and mood. Some verbs may be used more than once. Some blanks may require compound tenses.

aprender	comprar	dar
decidir	enseñar	estar
haber	hacer	ir
gozar	gustar	llevar
manejar	marcar	molestar
necesitar	revisar	sacar
seguir	ser	tener
tomar		

Cuando yo tenía 21 años, nunca (1) _____ un carro; siempre (2) _____

un autobús o les pedía a mis amigos que me (3) _____ a los lugares que

más me (4) _____ frecuentar: la playa y el centro comercial. Cuando por

fin, yo (5) _____ comprarme un carro, todavía tenía miedo de que

(6) _____ un accidente o que, por alguna razón improvista, no

(7) _____ suficiente dinero en mi cuenta para mantenerlo. Me alegraba

mucho de que pronto (8) _____ de mucha libertad, o mejor dicho "mayor movilidad", pero los riesgos (9) _____ preocupándome. Les

rogué a unos amigos que me (10) _____ a manejar, así que

(11) _____ todos los sábados a un gran estacionamiento que, por ser de

una escuela, siempre (12) _____ vacío entonces. Bueno, después de unas

semanas, les gustó que yo (13) _____ a manejar. Así que

(14) luego _____ mi licencia. Ya era el momento de buscar un carro.

Quería un carro que (15) _____ grande y que (16) _____

transmisión automática. Me importaba que no (17) _____ muchas millas

y que no (18) _____ reparaciones urgentes. Me (19) _____

cuenta de que era preciso que yo (20) _____ el carro de una persona

que (21) _____ honesta y a quien no le (22) _____ que un

mecánico lo (23) _____ antes de que nosotros (24) _____ el

trato. En fin, todo salió bien y compré un carro con pocas millas, en buenas

condiciones, de ocho cilindros, cuatro puertas y que (25) _____

suficiente espacio para mi equipo de pescar.

Multiple choice. Select the clauses that correctly complete the sentences.

1. Muchos viven como si lo que compran _____.
   a. no hace ningún impacto en el medio ambiente
   b. no hubo ningún impacto en el medio ambiente
   c. no hiciera ningún impacto en el medio ambiente
   d. no haga ningún impacto en el medio ambiente

2. Vamos a seguir usando petróleo hasta que _____.
   a. se nos acabó
   b. se nos acabe
   c. se nos acababa
   d. se nos acabara

3. Es urgente que _____.
   a. ahorremos los recursos naturales
   b. ahorramos los recursos naturales
   c. ahorráramos los recursos naturales
   d. ahorrábamos los recursos naturales

4. Me recomendaron que _____.
   a. recicla productos de plástico, vidrio y metal
   b. recicle productos de plástico, vidrio y metal
   c. reciclaba productos de plástico, vidrio y metal
   d. reciclara productos de plástico, vidrio y metal

5. Por favor, acompáñame al mercado de productos orgánicos
   una vez que _____.
   a. habrás separado los reciclables de la basura
   b. hubieras separado los reciclables de la basura
   c. hayas separado los reciclables de la basura
   d. has separado los reciclables de la basura

6. Es necesario que todos nosotros _____.
   a. ayudemos a proteger las especies en peligro de extinción
   b. ayudamos a proteger las especies en peligro de extinción
   c. ayudábamos a proteger las especies en peligro de extinción
   d. ayudáramos a proteger las especies en peligro de extinción

7. El cáncer de la piel va a seguir siendo cada vez frecuente
   mientras que _____.
   a. la capa de ozono sigue disminuyéndose
   b. la capa de ozono siguiera disminuyéndose
   c. la capa de ozono siga disminuyéndose
   d. la capa de ozono seguirá disminuyéndose

8. Muchos temen que _____.
   a. el nivel del mar va a subir de manera alarmante
   b. el nivel del mar iba a subir de manera alarmante
   c. el nivel del mar fuera a subir de manera alarmante
   d. el nivel del mar vaya a subir de manera alarmante

9. Aunque ayer los políticos _____.
   a. hablen, no hacen nada para salvar el planeta
   b. hablan, no hacen nada para salvar el planeta
   c. hablarán, no hacen nada para salvar el planeta
   d. hablaban, no hacían nada para salvar el planeta

10. El sector energético requiere fuentes de energía que _____.
    a. son sostenibles
    b. sean sostenibles
    c. eran sostenibles
    d. fueran sostenibles

11. Era horroroso que _____.
    a. el uso de pesticidas y herbicidas cause defectos genéticos
    b. el uso de pesticidas y herbicidas causa defectos genéticos
    c. el uso de pesticidas y herbicidas causara defectos genéticos
    d. el uso de pesticidas y herbicidas causaba defectos genéticos

12. No cabía duda de que _____.
    a. las capas de hielo polares estén deteriorándose
    b. las capas de hielo polares estuvieran deteriorándose
    c. las capas de hielo polares estaban deteriorándose
    d. las capas de hielo polares están deteriorándose

13. Hay ciertas personas que niegan que _____.
    a. el efecto invernadero es un hecho comprobado por científicos internacionales
    b. el efecto invernadero sea un hecho comprobado por científicos internacionales
    c. el efecto invernadero era un hecho comprobado por científicos internacionales
    d. el efecto invernadero será un hecho comprobado por científicos internacionales

14. Es cierto que _____.
    a. la energía solar y térmica no contaminan
    b. la energía solar y térmica no contaminen
    c. la energía solar y térmica no contaminaran
    d. la energía solar y térmica no contaminaban

15. Dijo un científico que era importante que _____.
    a. el gobierno protege la biodiversidad
    b. el gobierno protegía la biodiversidad
    c. el gobierno proteja la biodiversidad
    d. el gobierno protegiera la biodiversidad

16. Buscábamos las granjas que _____.
    a. cultivaran vegetales orgánicos
    b. cultivan vegetales orgánicos
    c. cultivaban vegetales orgánicos
    d. cultiven vegetales orgánicos

17. Es verdad que _____.
    a. Cuba goce de un clima paradisíaco
    b. Cuba gozaba de un clima paradisíaco
    c. Cuba goza de un clima paradisíaco
    d. Cuba gozará de un clima paradisíaco

18. Le pareció imposible que _____.
    a. hubiera tantos desechos de plástico en los mares
    b. hay tantos desechos de plástico en los mares
    c. había tantos desechos de plástico en los mares
    d. hubo tantos desechos de plástico en los mares

19. Se necesitan medios de transporte público que _____.
    a. no dependen del petróleo
    b. no dependan del petróleo
    c. no dependerán del petróleo
    d. no dependían del petróleo

20. Alguien dijo que el mundo se va a acabar a menos que _____.
    a. a alguien como tú le importa mucho salvarlo
    b. a alguien como tú le importaba mucho salvarlo
    c. a alguien como tú le importe mucho salvarlo
    d. a alguien como tú le importara mucho salvarlo

EJERCICIO
7·25

Fill in the blanks with the correct form of the verbs in parentheses.

1. Según el pronóstico, es probable que mañana _____ un día parcialmente nublado. (ser)

2. No me gusta que la temporada ciclónica _____ pronto. (comenzar)

3. Quiero tener una aplicación con que _____ ver el tiempo en vivo. (poder)

4. No es cierto que el cambio de las mareas _____ precisamente cada seis horas. (ocurrir)

5. Fue una lástima que la marejada _____ el Hotel del Malecón. (destruir)

6. Vamos a pescar cuando _____ la presión atmosférica. (bajar)

7. Los esquiadores esperan que _____ mucho en las montañas esta noche. (nevar)

8. Ella no duda que el efecto invernadero no _____ un fraude sino un hecho comprobado. (ser)

9. Es peligroso manejar si la temperatura baja cuando _____. (llover)

10. Es posible que la velocidad de los vientos _____ los 200 km/hora. (alcanzar)

11. Siempre nos gusta tomar el sol cuando _____ un día despejado. (tener)

12. Los niños se asustaron cuando _____ los truenos. (oír)

13. Ponemos el carro en el garaje en caso de que _____ mucha nieve. (caer)

14. Puse cadenas en las llantas para que el carro no se _____. (resbalar)

15. Su mamá le dijo que se _____ el impermeable porque iba a llover. (poner)

16. Los animales se asustarán cuando _____ los truenos. (oír)

17. Todos se sorprenderían en Seattle si no _____ en enero. (llover)

18. No era una buena idea dejar que los niños _____ sin ponerse un suéter. (salir)

19. Antes de que el huracán _____ tierra, lograron evacuar las ciudades costeñas. (tocar)

20. Todos se alegran de que por fin _____ llovido en el sur de California. (haber)

Translate the following sentences from Spanish to English.

1. La mesera nos sirvió los postres antes de que hubiéramos dejado de comer.

   _____

2. Es importante que el equipo limpie el derrame de líquido biopeligroso.

   _____

3. Van a salir después de que hayamos visto la película.

   _____

4. Ella necesitaba un carro que no usara mucho petróleo.

   _____

5. El piloto espera aterrizar antes de que llueva.

   _____

6. Doctor, cuando ella se despierte, llámeme, por favor.

   _____

7. Ella quiere que él deposite los fondos en la cuenta de ahorros de ella.

   _____

8. Preferimos un cuarto que tenga un balcón con vista a la playa.

   _____

9. Le dije a la enfermera que le trajera otra almohada para mi mamá.

   _____

10. Me dejaron cambiar ese vino por éste aunque yo no tenía el recibo.

   _____

Translate the following sentences from English to Spanish.

1. Unless the customer has a receipt, we cannot give her a cash refund.

   _____

2. It bothered him that his screen kept freezing up.

   _____

3. His father wanted a truck that had a CD player.

   _____

4. I asked them to replace my keyboard.

   _____

5. My mother should have eaten foods that had less fat and sodium.

   _____

6. It's incredible that some people don't believe scientists.

   _____

7. The children hope it stops raining soon so they can go out and play.

   _____

8. The engineers were happy that their design had been accepted.

   _____

9. Is there an application that allows me to transfer funds from one bank to another?

   _____

10. There was no one in the store who knew how to repair my cellphone.

    _____

Answer key

Keep in mind when checking your work in the translation exercises that as long as your solutions mean the same thing as the sentences given in the key, you are doing fine. It is inevitable that translations may vary, since meaning is more important than the exact words. When any doubt remains, focus on your rendition of the verbs.

1   When to use the subjunctive and how to form its four tenses

1·1
1. piense
2. creáis
3. diga
4. tengamos
5. vea
6. sea
7. haya
8. vayas
9. den
10. duerma
11. conozca
12. sepas
13. conduzca
14. hagan
15. escribáis
16. saque
17. pague
18. empiece
19. concluyamos
20. estén

1·2

1. estuvieras
2. supieran
3. pusiéramos
4. pudiera
5. murieran
6. tuviera
7. vieran
8. diera
9. fuera
10. hubieran
11. viera
12. fuera
13. pagaras
14. anduvierais
15. hiciera
16. trabajara
17. condujera
18. leyeran
19. hablárais
20. comieras

1·3

1. haya cubierto
2. haya escrito
3. hayáis hablado
4. hayas visto
5. haya muerto
6. haya dormido
7. hayáis comido
8. haya abierto
9. hayamos hecho
10. hayan comido
11. haya sabido
12. haya dicho
13. hayas ido
14. haya vivido

15. haya cubierto
16. hayáis venido
17. hayan puesto
18. hayas conocido
19. haya roto
20. haya conducido

1·4
1. hubiera cantado
2. hubiera abierto
3. hubiera visto
4. hubiéramos destruido
5. hubieran obtenido
6. hubiera castigado
7. hubieras verificado
8. hubieran sistematizado
9. hubierais descubierto
10. hubiera conocido
11. hubieran hecho
12. hubiera mentido
13. hubierais conducido
14. hubieras servido
15. hubiera fabricado
16. hubiéramos pedido
17. hubiera sobornado
18. hubiera roto
19. hubiera dicho
20. hubieras escrito

2 Sequence of tenses and the subjunctive

2·1
1. tenga
2. vieras
3. vayan
4. leyeran
5. pague

6. hablaran

7. hubiera traducido

8. hayas escrito

9. diga

10. escucháramos

11. trabaje

12. hubiera renunciado

2·2   1. b

2. g

3. c

4. f

5. h

6. i

7. j

8. d

9. e

10. a

2·3   1. c. *The main verb is in the present and thus requires the present subjunctive to be used.*

2. a. *Compare this sentence with the previous one and note that the only difference between them is found in the different tenses of the verb in their respective main clauses. Thus, according to the rules of sequence, the past subjunctive must be used.*

3. b. *From a structural point of view, this sentence is identical to the previous one. Only the subjects and verbs have been changed, demonstrating the efficacy of a slot-and-substitution approach to the subjunctive, with model sentences for the various situations in which it is used.*

4. b. *The main verb is in the present tense. The other options, although subjunctives, are in the imperfect subjunctive (past).*

5. c. *Once again, the main verb is in the present tense.*

6. c. *The main verb is in the past (imperfect indicative). If you got this one wrong, be sure you were not led astray by the use of the plural in the subordinate clause—it is irrelevant to your choice since each option states their subjects (todos, pobres). The correct answer is not correct because of the person and number of the verb, but because of the correct use of the sequence of tenses. The others, although subjunctive, are all in the present tense.*

7. b. *The main verb is preterite and therefore the imperfect subjunctive must be used.*

8. a. *The main verb is present and therefore the present subjunctive must be used.*

9. b. *The main verb is present and therefore the present subjunctive must be used.*

10. b. *The main verb is present and therefore the present subjunctive must be used.*

3 Subordinated noun clauses

3·1

1. piense *If he thinks of her as a matter of habit, is doing so now, or is going to be thinking of her, then the present subjunctive is the solution. However, if he has been doing so up to the moment this sentence was uttered, the present perfect subjunctive would be necessary:* haya pensado. *The subordinated clause is introduced by an impersonal expression of emotion.*

2. hablaban *The impersonal expression is one of observation, not doubt.*

3. vieras *If we were hoping you were going to see it, then the imperfect subjunctive would be used. However, if we were hoping you already had seen it, then the pluperfect subjunctive would be required:* hubieras visto.

4. vengan *If the party has not yet taken place, only the present subjunctive would be possible here, because the emotion is present about a future action. If the party were in progress, it would have required the present perfect subjunctive:* hayan venido.

5. vaya *The present subjunctive is required, if she's thinking about his going at the moment she speaks, or very soon thereafter. However, if he has already left, the present perfect subjunctive would be required:* haya ido.

6. pueda *If you're currently doubting my abilities to eat the whole cake, the present subjunctive is required. But if I'm taking credit for an empty plate, it would require the present perfect subjunctive,* haya podido, *because it would refer to an action that has taken place and whose effect (the empty plate) is still being noticed.*

7. alquilara *The imperfect subjunctive is required because the main verb is in a past tense.*

8. haya vivido *The present perfect subjunctive is needed because the question is whether he ever has lived there. The subjunctive is needed because of doubt. The need for the present perfect as opposed to any other subjunctive is found in the use of the temporal clue* jamás.

9. pueda *The present subjunctive is needed if we doubt their abilities in a new case. However, if it were an old case, or if they'd been working unsuccessfully, the present perfect would be required:* haya podido.

10. traduzca *The present subjunctive is required because someone is telling someone to ask someone else to do something. Commands and requests do not allow for any other time frame than the future, because it is impossible to ask or tell someone to have done anything already. This reveals that the present subjunctive extends to the future.*

11. sepan *The doubt is in the present, hence the present subjunctive must be used in the subordinated clause. Other time frames are conceivable, but more context would be required to justify any other answer.*

12. llevaba *The imperfect indicative, not the subjunctive, must be used in this subordinated clause because the main clause contains a verb of belief.*

3·2

1. h
2. b
3. a
4. e
5. f

6. g

7. c

8. j

9. d

10. i

3·3

1. c. *The main verb is a verb of requesting and is in the present tense; therefore the present subjunctive is required in the subordinated clause.*

2. c. *The main verb is a verb of wanting and is in the imperfect indicative, a past tense, and therefore the imperfect subjunctive is required in the subordinated clause.*

3. b. *The main verb is a verb of insisting in the imperfect indicative; therefore the imperfect subjunctive is required in the subordinated clause.*

4. a. *The verb of the main clause is* molestó, *a verb of emotion in the preterite, a past tense. It is not* leía. *Nonetheless, the information in the time clause reveals that the speaker was reading a newspaper—a medium that reports past events. Therefore, the speaker's annoyance, in the past, is about an event that had happened previously, which makes the pluperfect subjunctive necessary.*

5. b. *The verb of the main clause is in the present and is a verb of belief, not disbelief or doubt. Therefore, the subjunctive is not to be used in the subordinated clause.*

6. a. *The verb of the main clause is a verb of wanting in the imperfect; therefore the imperfect subjunctive is required in the subordinated clause.*

7. c. *The verb of the main clause is a verb of requesting in the present; therefore the present subjunctive is required in the subordinated clause.*

8. d. *The main verb is* dijo, *used as a verb of commanding; therefore the imperfect subjunctive is required in the subordinated clause.*

9. c. *The verb of the main clause is a verb of hoping or expecting in the present; therefore the present subjunctive is required in the subordinated clause.*

10. b. *The verb of the main clause is a verb of observation, mere reporting, in the imperfect; therefore the subjunctive must not be used in the subordinated clause. The logic of sequence must still be observed and therefore the imperfect indicative must be used in the subordinated clause.*

3·4

1. It's important to give John the news as soon as possible.

2. Our parents hoped we would be successful in life.

3. Tell them not to go to that beach because it is very polluted.

4. It was imperative that they serve the food on time (*or* for them to serve . . .).

5. I doubt that you know much about Babylonian astronomy.

6. We did not believe that she had studied the lesson before coming to class.

7. Doctors recommend that we get at least seven hours of sleep.

8. It is going to be very important for you to be able to use the subjunctive if you want to go to Mexico.

9. She doubted that he wanted her to go with him to the party.

10. I couldn't believe that Susan had investigated me before asking me for the list.

3·5

1. Sus amigos le pidieron que trajera su cámara digital a la fiesta.
2. Esperábamos que ella consiguiera un nuevo novio (*or* que ella encontrara otro novio).
3. Ellos (*or* Ellas) querían que él se fuera (*or* que él saliera).
4. ¿Esperas que la ópera comience pronto? (*or* empiece)
5. Sus padres se alegran de que ella se haya casado con Mateo.
6. ¿Es necesario que paguemos la comida aquí?
7. Sus jefes esperaban que ella grabara todas las llamadas telefónicas.
8. La policía pidió que la gente buscara el perro extraviado.
9. ¿Se alegra Ud. de que ella fuera a Europa? (*or* ¿Te alegras…?)
10. ¿Se enojaron de que ella hubiera vuelto temprano? (*or* hubiera regresado)

3·6

1. me puse
2. supe
3. hubiera
4. enfadó/ofendió
5. hubiera
6. había
7. dudaba
8. respaldaran
9. había
10. eran
11. enfadó/ofendió
12. acusara
13. obligaran
14. eran
15. tenía
16. había
17. castigaran
18. había
19. pidieran

4 Subordinated adjective clauses

4·1
1. sea
2. tenga
3. sepa
4. escribía
5. cantara
6. pudiera
7. vaya
8. entregó
9. tradujera
10. empiece
11. tuviera
12. paguen

4·2
1. f
2. e
3. i
4. j
5. a
6. d
7. h
8. g
9. c
10. b

4·3
1. c. *The antecedent is* personas, *who are unspecified, which requires the subjunctive to be used in the subordinated clause; the time frame is in the past, so the imperfect subjunctive must be used.*

2. a. *The antecedent is* jefes. *The use of* aquellos *labels them as a type or class of bosses, but does not go any further with a specific identification, such as a name would, and therefore they are unspecified, or vague. The subjunctive is therefore required in the subordinated clause. Because the time frame is past, the imperfect subjunctive must be used. Note that in practice, a speaker might be engaged in a conversation in which the bosses are known to both speaker and listener and would therefore refer to known individuals. If this were the case, the indicative would be required, or, more precisely, it would indicate that the speaker is referring to known individuals.*

3. b. *The antecedent is* persona, *as a type of person, not a specific person. The subjunctive must therefore be used in the subordinated clause. The use of the present makes a general assertion, and therefore the present subjunctive is used.*

4. b. *The antecedent is* mujeres, *referred to as a type that Casanova preferred (worldly ones), not to any being identified, and therefore the subjunctive is required. The time frame being past, the imperfect subjunctive is used.*

5. d. *The antecedent is* entrenador. *Because the team is hoping to get one, he is as yet unidentified (don't be led astray by the use of* tener *in this case), and therefore the subjunctive is required in the subordinated clause. The present time frame requires the use of the present subjunctive.*

6. b. *The antecedent,* libro, *is one being sought, and therefore as yet unidentified. The subjunctive is required. The present time frame requires the present subjunctive.*

7. c. *The antecedent is* universidad, *a certain type of which was still being sought by her parents. Therefore, the imperfect subjunctive is required in the subordinated clause. Note that even though everyone knows that such a university exists, the context of the sentence is that the parents had not yet identified one of that type. The lesson here is to not think, or make assumptions, beyond the information actually stated in the sentence, even when the sentence is of one's own creation.*

8. a. *The antecedent is* muñeca. *Although the verb* buscar *is used, the use of the definite article* la *reveals that the little girls know exactly which doll they are looking for (one they have mislaid or one they may have seen in a toy store). The indicative is therefore required in the subordinated clause.*

9. b. *The antecedent is* lago, *but it is one that the speaker asserts did not exist at some time in the past. Therefore, the imperfect subjunctive is required in the subordinated clause.*

10. b. *The antecedent is* novela, *one of a class, not a specific title. That fact and the present time frame make the present subjunctive required in the subordinated clause.*

4·4

1. The engineers needed to find a solution that wasn't so costly.

2. We preferred to listen to music that would not make us nervous.

3. The musicians have guitars that sound good.

4. The astronaut wanted to have a boyfriend who would be faithful to her.

5. There is no clothing by those designers that is practical.

6. I am not interested in the books that are sold at the supermarket checkout.

7. One day we hope to live in a house that has a big garage.

8. I wanted to buy a sailboat that could sail very fast.

9. There is no man who can equal Don Juan in gambling, in dueling, or in love.

10. I have a flashlight that lights up a great part of the road.

4·5

1. Necesitaban una mesa que fuera más grande.

2. Queremos hallar una ciudad que tenga menos crimen.

3. No había ni un muchacho allí a quien no le gustaran los deportes.

4. Él y yo buscábamos un diccionario que incluyera términos de mecánica.

5. Quiero un jardín que solamente tenga flores azules.

6. Él quiere votar por el candidato que tiene las mejores ideas.

7. Él espera encontrar un candidato que sea honesto.

8. Ellos (*or* Ellas) buscaban un mapa que indicara los parques.

9. ¿Quieres ir a una playa que tenga mesas para comidas campestres?

10. Encontramos un carro usado que tenía llantas nuevas.

5   Adverbial expressions

5·1

1. invirtió

2. vendas

3. contraten *Or, if the speaker asserts that he knows that the company has hired experts, the present perfect subjunctive,* hayan contratado, *would be used; or, if the company is hiring experts, the present progressive (with the subjunctive of the helping verb),* estén contratando, *would be used.*

4. empacara

5. diga

6. trajo *A mere report of a past event.*

7. se pongan

8. conozca

9. trajera

10. romper

11. recibiéramos

12. enviarle

5·2

1. d

2. i

3. h

4. g

5. m

6. j

7. l

8. a

9. k

10. o

11. f

12. n

13. b

14. e

15. c

5·3   1. b. *The phrase* antes de que *always requires the subjunctive, and since the main verb,* dejaron, *is in the preterite, a past tense, the imperfect subjunctive is required.*

2. c. *The phrase* a pesar de que *sometimes requires the subjunctive, but that is not the case in this instance. It is a mere report of a past action; no anticipation is involved.*

3. b. *The subjunctive is not used after* mientras *if it is used to introduce a report of past action; in other words, when the action following it is not anticipated. Because the two actions of reading and doing homework were contemporaneous, both are in the imperfect indicative.*

4. c. *The phrase* de manera que *is used as a purpose clause and therefore requires the subjunctive. Because the main verb is past (imperfect indicative), the imperfect subjunctive must be used.*

5. a. *The time frame is clearly present, as evidenced by the use of both the present tense and the word* ahora. *The cue* tal vez, *along with the implication of the possibility of rain later, makes the present subjunctive necessary.*

6. a. *The time frame is future, as shown by* va a casarse, *the verb phrase in the main clause. The phrase* con tal de que *is a phrase of proviso and is always followed by the subjunctive.*

7. d. *The use of* hicieron *establishes the past time frame and because* para que *is a purpose clause that always must be followed by the subjunctive, the imperfect subjunctive must be used.*

8. d. *The time frame is future, as shown by the use of* van a dar *(the future formed from* ir a + *infinitive). The phrase* siempre que *requires the subjunctive in this case because of the anticipation created by the use of* ir a *in the main clause.*

9. c. *Commands are always in the present time frame; therefore, the phrase* hasta que *introduces a future action and thus it is anticipated—and the present subjunctive must be used.*

10. b. *The time frame is present and because the phrase* siempre y cuando *is a statement of proviso and requires the subjunctive, the present subjunctive must be used.*

5·4   1. It was important to finish the road before they began the walls.

2. The young woman refused to knit the sweater unless her boyfriend bought her the yarn.

3. There were a lot of people in the park despite the fact it was raining.

4. They fixed the project's model so it would look more realistic.

5. The teenagers were eating as if they had gone days without a bite.

6. The thieves left the bank without anyone seeing them.

7. They are going to place an ad in the newspaper so that more people will apply for the job.

8. They read the novel from cover to cover so that they could discuss it.

9. I am going to go out as soon as I finish this chapter.

10. The boss was going to write us a check unless there were no funds in the account.

5·5
1. El equipo se acostará temprano para poder jugar mejor mañana.

2. Él va a ganar, aunque este año no lo ha hecho bien (*or* no ha jugado bien).

3. Ellos (*or* Ellas) van a estudiar física a menos que su profesor les recomiende otra clase.

4. Una vez que ella había subido la montaña, pudo ver el océano (*or* el mar).

5. Te veré cuando llegues.

6. Por mucho que practicamos ayer, no pudimos aprender el juego.

7. Aunque escriba bien, el editor no la va a contratar.

8. Una vez que llegues a El Paso, cruzar a Ciudad Juárez es fácil.

9. Los niños iban a jugar con el perro, con tal de que su madre les permitiera hacerlo.

10. Él y yo vamos a jugar al ajedrez, aunque generalmente él gana.

6 Contrary-to-fact statements

6·1
1. C
2. H
3. H
4. C
5. H
6. H
7. C
8. C
9. C
10. H
11. C
12. H

6·2
1. acompañaríamos
2. diría
3. hubiera dicho
4. irían
5. tradujeran
6. pudiera

7. tuviéramos/pondríamos
8. tendría
9. ganaran
10. saldría
11. dirías
12. hubiera sabido

6·3
1. Those children will never learn if they keep reading comics.
2. John's father would give him a car if he were more responsible.
3. What would happen if no one wanted to go to war?
4. If elephants could fly, the streets of the world would be very dirty.
5. If there is no food in the house, we will have to go buy it (*or* some).
6. If you dedicated more time to your studies, you would be able to pass your classes.
7. We would have more money if we did not spend it on stupid things.
8. My friends in Tibet would call me if they had a cellular phone.
9. If politicians did not waste our money, we would be richer.
10. If I spend more time on the subjunctive, I will be able to use it without difficulty.

6·4
1. ¿Qué harías si tuvieras tanto dinero como Bill Gates?
2. Sus amigos habrían venido (*or* hubieran venido) si él les hubiera dicho que había una fiesta.
3. Si tienes tiempo mañana, iremos al cine.
4. Nos quedaremos en casa esta noche si llueve.
5. Si ella admitiera que mintió, me sentiría mejor.
6. Manejaré si lees el mapa.
7. ¿Irías al planeta Marte si NASA te diera la oportunidad?
8. Yo aprendería a tocar el piano si tuviera tiempo.
9. Si ellos (*or* ellas) hubieran asistido a la conferencia, nosotros les habríamos causado una buena impresión (*or* hubiéramos causado).
10. Ella convencería a su jefe si él pudiera entenderla.

6·5
1. A. Si invertimos en esos valores, ganaremos mucho.
   B. Si invirtiéramos en esos valores, ganaríamos mucho.
2. A. Ellos venderán la compañía si la junta de directores no se opone a ello.
   B. Ellos venderían la compañía si la junta de directores no se opusiera a ello.

3. A. Si ella trae la comida, iremos a la playa.

   B. Si ella trajera la comida, iríamos a la playa.

4. A. Llamaré al mecánico si el carro no funciona bien.

   B. Llamaría al mecánico si el carro no funcionara bien.

5. A. Si ella desea (*or* Si ella quiere) comprar el carro, su padre le dará el dinero.

   B. Si ella deseara (*or* Si ella quisiera) comprar el carro, su padre le daría el dinero.

6. A. Aun si ella quiere (*or* si ella desea) comprar una acción, a él no le gustará.

   B. Aun si ella quisiera (*or* si ella deseara) comprar una acción, a él no le gustaría.

7. A. Si el general se lo manda, las tropas atacarán.

   B. Si el general se lo mandara, las tropas atacarían.

8. A. Lloverá si hace calor.

   B. Llovería si hiciera calor.

9. A. Morirán si intentan nadar en el río (*or* si tratan de nadar).

   B. Morirían si intentaran nadar en el río (or si trataran de nadar).

10. A. ¡Si lo haces (*or* Si lo vuelves a hacer) otra vez, me quejaré con el gerente!

    B. ¡Si lo hicieras (*or* Si lo volvieras a hacer) otra vez, me quejaría con el gerente!

11. A. Si ellos llevan su perro a la fiesta, no lo dejaré entrar.

    B. Si ellos llevaran su perro a la fiesta, no lo dejaría entrar.

12. A. Él asistirá a la universidad, aun si sus padres no tienen suficiente dinero.

    B. Él asistiría a la universidad, aun si sus padres no tuvieran suficiente dinero.

13. A. Los contrataremos si no nos piden demasiado.

    B. Los contrataríamos si no nos pidieran demasiado.

14. A. Él devolverá la mercancía si ella tiene el comprobante.

    B. Él devolvería la mercancía si ella tuviera el comprobante.

15. A. Si me voy, ellos no sabrán qué hacer.

    B. Si me fuera, ellos no sabrían qué hacer.

7   Comprehensive exercises

7·1
1. estuviera *Adverbial clause, past time frame.*

2. sepan *Adjective clause, present time frame.*

3. haga *Adjective clause, present time frame.*

4. pudiera *Adverbial clause, past time frame.*

5. volver

6. se durmiera *Noun clause, past time frame.*

7. llega

8. fueran *Adjective clause, past time frame.*

9. den *Noun clause, present time frame.*

10. conozco

11. pidieran *Adjective clause, past time frame.*

12. produjera *Adjective clause, past time frame.*

13. pagar

14. pregunte *Noun clause, present time frame.*

15. contó *or* había contado (*even* contara – *see p. 18*) *Adverbial clause, past time frame.*

16. dijera *Adverbial clause, past time frame.*

17. miraba

18. repite

19. piensen *Adjective clause, present time frame.*

20. había leído (*or* leí)

21. hubiera oído *Contrary-to-fact statement, past time frame.*

22. supieran *Adjective clause, past time frame.*

23. hayas traído *However, if the group were no longer at the beach,* hubieras traído. *Noun clause of emotion, but referring either to immediate past time or a more remote past time (haven't brought or hadn't brought).*

24. dé *Noun clause, present time frame.*

25. se pongan *Adverbial clause, present time frame.*

7·2

1. i
2. j
3. h
4. g
5. c
6. d
7. e
8. b
9. f
10. a

7·3

1. e
2. g
3. f

4. h

5. d

6. c

7. b

8. j

9. a

10. i

7·4

1. c. *The phrase* a menos que *is an adverbial one that always requires the subjunctive. The time frame is present.*

2. d. *The impersonal expression* es fenomenal *is one of emotion, in the present, and introduces a subordinated noun clause.*

3. c. *The phrase* para que *is an adverbial clause expressing purpose and always requires the subjunctive. The timeframe is past.*

4. c. *The past time frame is established twice, and the main clause contains a verb of emotion, introducing a subordinated noun clause.*

5. c. *The adverb* hasta *does not introduce a clause. It is a preposition and can only be followed by an infinitive. If* que *followed* hasta, *then it would require the present subjunctive.*

6. c. *The expression* una vez que *is an adverbial time phrase with the meaning "once" followed by the expression of something happening (e.g., "Once the kids go to bed, we'll have some quiet"). Here it is introduced by a verb of promising in the past; therefore, there is an element of anticipation at the moment the promise was made. It does not matter whether in the moment the sentence is spoken, the promise has or has not been fulfilled. What matters is the observance of the rule of sequence of tenses; therefore, the imperfect subjunctive must be used.*

7. d. *The verb of recommending, in the past, introduces a subordinated noun clause whose verb must therefore be in the imperfect subjunctive.*

8. b. *This is an example of a subordinated adjective clause, introduced by a main clause in the past. The antecedent* perro *was nonspecific; therefore, the imperfect subjunctive must be used.*

9. a. *The adverbial expression* hasta que *needs to be followed by the present subjunctive in this case because the future time frame established by* seguiré esperando *creates anticipation for whatever action follows.*

10. a. *When the adverb* cuando *is preceded by a verb in the present, just as in the case of* mientras, *the action following it is anticipated and the present subjunctive must be used.*

11. a. *There is nothing in this sentence that requires the subjunctive, but it is a good reminder that two simultaneous, ongoing actions in the past will both be expressed by the imperfect indicative.*

12. c. *The verb of doubt in the past introduces a subordinated noun clause and hence the imperfect subjunctive must be used.*

13. b. *Compare this with number 10, above. This example shows how it is possible to encounter sentences using* cuando *in a past sequence in which an action was anticipated, and in which the imperfect subjunctive will be required.*

14. c. *The impersonal expression of emotion in the past introduces a subordinated noun clause, hence the imperfect subjunctive must be used.*

15. c. *The past time frame is established by* no le molestó, *but it is not the reason for the subjunctive being used in the subordinated clause. The phrase* siempre que *is a statement of proviso, and as such creates anticipation, hence the subjunctive.*

16. b. *The temporal adverbial expression* tan pronto como, *in a present time frame, creates anticipation, hence the present subjunctive is used.*

17. b. *The adverbial expression* a no ser que *must always be followed by the subjunctive; the present time frame requires that it be the present subjunctive.*

18. d. *The verb of the main clause is a verb of belief, so the subjunctive must not be used in the subordinated clause. Nonetheless, the sequence of tenses must be observed and therefore the imperfect indicative is used.*

19. a. *The adverbial expression* como si *must always be followed by either the imperfect subjunctive or the pluperfect subjunctive. Because the mountain climbers had to have been born before they scaled the summit, the pluperfect subjunctive must be used.*

20. b. *The main verb is a verb of emotion, in the present, and introduces a subordinated noun clause. Because the action referred to is a prior purchase whose influence is still being felt, the present perfect subjunctive must be used.*

7·5

1. The couple got married before they kissed at the altar.
2. You hope that I don't expect you to wait for me.
3. I was looking for you everywhere, hoping that you were missing me.
4. The fishermen launched their sailboats into the sea, despite the rain.
5. If all mothers-in-law died, husbands would be worth more.
6. The kids were hoping that Saint Nick would bring them a lot of toys.
7. The young man is going to ask her to dance as soon as he sees her.
8. He came to the USA hoping he would have better luck.
9. The flying saucer disappeared as quickly as it had appeared.
10. I decided that I would play pool with Juan as soon as he could get to the bar.
11. There wasn't a single book in the bookstore that dealt with the subject that interested me.
12. —Are you going shopping? —Yes, even though my parents have not given me much money.
13. The politicians wanted to give it all away to corrupt contractors.
14. Do you prefer music with good lyrics to that which is danceable?
15. After you leave the house is not the time to wonder whether you have turned off the oven.

16. They think they're going to Acapulco, provided there is a cheap flight this weekend.

17. Do you want to go with her to the cafeteria or do you prefer that she go alone?

18. We need a person who knows Swahili and who can teach it.

19. Juana wanted a ring that was more elegant and hoped that Juan would buy it for her.

20. That teenager only wants a girlfriend who will do what interests him.

7·6

1. Era una lástima que su esposo la hubiera abandonado con todos esos hijos.

2. Los pilotos esperaban que los asistentes de vuelo sirvieran la cena.

3. La niñita no comerá la sopa de los osos a menos que tenga mucha hambre.

4. Sus maestros siempre le decían que se metiera de lleno en los estudios.

5. Cuando buceaban, tenían miedo de lo que verían.

6. Si ella fue a la fiesta, pues, él la vio, pero dudo que ella fuera.

7. Si la rechazan una vez más, creo que va a llorar.

8. Cuando él oyó las noticias, dudó que le hubieran dicho la verdad.

9. Los osos estaban enojados porque la niñita había comido la sopa de ellos.

10. No hubo/había nadie que se entristeciera cuando murió Susana.

11. Si fueras a Cuba, ¿a cuáles/qué lugares visitarías?

12. Después de comer, los animales se durmieron.

13. Ellos (*or* Ellas) esperaban que él llegara antes de que anocheciera/antes de anochecer.

14. Antes de aprender (*or* Antes de que aprendiera...) a manejar, ella nunca quería hacer nada.

15. Una vez que hayas terminado este libro, podrás usar el subjuntivo correctamente.

16. ¿Crees que a alguien le importaría si ellos tuvieran mala suerte?

17. Si pudieras vendérnoslo por menos, pediríamos más.

18. Si quieres paz, es necesario luchar por la justicia (*or* que luches por la justicia).

19. A no ser por tus padres (*or* Si no hubiera sido por tus padres...), no estarías aquí.

20. No te olvides de cerrar la puerta después de entrar o salir del edificio.

7·7

1. se conocieran

2. vivían

3. se casaron

4. gustara

5. se crió (*or* se había criado)

6. quiso

7. llevaran

8. tuvieran

9. fueran

10. tuvieran

11. asistieran

12. nací

13. decidieron

14. siguiera

15. terminara

16. pudiera

17. fue

18. se graduó

19. pagaba

20. hubiera graduado

7·8

1. fuera

2. sacaba

3. manejara

4. tendría

5. hacía

6. hiciera

7. se acordaba

8. pidieran

9. hiciera

10. prestara

11. usara

12. hubiera preparado

13. estuviera

14. hubiera limpiado

15. estuviera

16. empezara

17. dejara

18. tuviera

19. fuera

20. fuera

7·9   1. son

2. incluya

3. tenga

4. tenga

5. se congele

6. venga

7. mida

8. se congela

9. ocurre

10. cueste

11. encuentre

12. pagara

13. vaya

14. pida

15. revele

16. quiero

17. estuvieras

18. harías

19. recomiendas (*or* ¿Qué me recomendarías que hiciera?)

20. haga

7·10   1. dieran

2. dijeron

3. llenara

4. leyera

5. había recetado

6. tuvieran

7. hubiera indicado

8. era

9. tomara

10. visitaran

11. eran

12. leyera

13. hicieran

14. captivaba

15. habían comido
16. vieran
17. pudieran
18. supo
19. dio
20. buscara

7·11
1. has preguntado
2. sería
3. hubiera sido inventado
4. habría
5. existieran/hubiera
6. podría
7. tendría
8. pudieras
9. inventarías
10. gustaría
11. dependiera
12. fuera
13. contara
14. serviría
15. construyeran
16. funcionaran
17. tenemos
18. hagamos
19. resuelva
20. vota

7·12
1. es
2. hubieran sucedido
3. sucedieron
4. lleva
5. sería
6. es
7. empleen

8. tener

9. congratularse

10. suele

11. trata

12. imagínese

13. pasaría

14. aplicara

15. tiene/guarda

16. se criaron

17. serían

18. hubiera nacido

19. guardara

20. valga

7·13

1. era

2. cumplió

3. decía

4. se casaría

5. pudiera

6. gustara/encantara/interesara

7. salía

8. decidió

9. fuera

10. buscaba

11. hubiera

12. encantaran/interesaran/gustaran

13. interesara/encantara/gustara

14. hablara

15. pudiera

16. fuera

17. conoció

18. se alegra

19. se casen

20. van

7·14   1. me quede

2. hace

3. brilla

4. vivamos

5. podamos

6. guste

7. pasemos

8. estudiemos

9. tengamos

10. pagan *(indicative, because the jobs are asserted as being the ones that pay little)*

11. me gradúe

12. siga

13. vaya

14. piensen

15. obtuviera

16. permitiera

17. sería

18. escuche

19. dependa

20. tenga

7.15   1. c. *The main verb is a verb of emotion expressed in a past tense (preterite); therefore the subjunctive must be used in the subordinated noun clause—and in the past. In this case, the pluperfect subjunctive, meaning* had arrived *because none of the verbs in the other options are in the subjunctive mood.*

2. a. *The verb introducing the subordinated noun clause (supimos) is not a WEIRDO verb. The other choices are also in the wrong time frame. In addition to not being the verb that introduces the subordinated clause, the verb* llegar *is in the preterite and although it follows* cuando, *it expresses a mere report of a past action.*

3. d. *Note that* cuando vayas al extranjero *is not the clause that determines the form of the options. It is a temporal clause, in the form of a personal address, referring to some future travel that the person spoken to might make (hence the present subjunctive* vayas). *The main clause is an impersonal expression, either general or simply in the present, about a requirement for travel. Option (b) completes the idea introduced by the main clause in a personal way, requiring a conjugated verb in the subjunctive in the subordinate noun clause—in the present subjunctive because the time frame is future. Option (c) completes the idea by continuing in the impersonal vein and thus uses the infinitive directly, without forming a subordinated noun clause.*

4. b. *The time frame is in the present, as revealed by the imperative; Ernesto's action is in the immediate future. Thus, the present subjunctive is needed after the adverbial expression* tan pronto como.

5. a. *The statement is a general one. The use of* siempre *eliminates any anticipation connected with this adverbial expression and therefore the verb must be in the indicative. Note that* me molesta—*a WEIRDO verb of emotion—does not govern the verb in the subordinated clause but, along with* siempre, *it does establish the time frame.*

6. b. *The main clause is one of emotion and requires the subjunctive in the subordinated noun clause. While the subject (*mamá*) could express her emotion about a past experience, the other options do not include subjunctive options (specifically,* hayamos hecho *or* hiciéramos*).*

7. a. *This is the option which is a hypothetical, or* if *clause. The prompt expresses a consequence about a contrary-to-fact situation in the past, hence the pluperfect subjunctive must be used.*

8. d. *The time frame is past (*llevaban… tenían*) and the main clause expresses an emotion, introducing a subordinated noun clause, hence the imperfect subjunctive is used.*

9. a. *The main clause expresses an emotion in the present, introducing a subordinated noun clause, and so the present subjunctive must be used. If you selected (b), thinking it was subjunctive, you may have forgotten that* permitir *is an -ir verb—a common error.*

10. c. *The main clause expresses a preference in the present, that someone else fulfills (in the subordinated noun clause) and therefore the verb must be in the present subjunctive.*

11. d. *The one-word main clause simply makes an observation; hence, the indicative must be used in the subordinated noun clause. All the other options are subjunctive.*

12. b. *The main clause expresses disbelief in the present time frame, introducing a subordinated noun clause in which the present subjunctive must be used.*

13. a. *The subordinated adjective clause modifies the type of airline the speaker is seeking, and thus* aerolínea *is a vague, non-specified antecedent and the present subjunctive must be used.*

14. b. *The subordinated noun clause is introduced in the main clause by a verb of forbidding in the present tense, requiring the present subjunctive in the subordinated clause. None of the other options are in the subjunctive mood.*

15. a. *The subjunctive is always required after the adverbial expression* antes de que. *Option (d) is also admissible, but less likely, since there is no context to justify it, such as would be the case if the sentence were more complex: "John fastened his seat belt before the plane had taken off when the overhead bin came open." To avoid verbal complications in "real life,"* el despegue, *a noun meaning "the take off," is frequently used, and so the clause would have avoided the subjunctive by saying "antes del despegue…". The other options, while all in the subjunctive mood, are in the wrong tenses.*

16. d. *The subjunctive is used after the adverbial clause* después de que *when the action is anticipated. Here, the time frame is present and future, and hence only the present subjunctive can be used. Option (c), while it is in the subjunctive mood, is in the past. The other options are indicative.*

17. a. *The subjunctive must be used in the subordinated adjective clause because the speaker does not know who will be on the flight crew and is not thinking of a specific person. The present subjunctive is needed due to the present time frame established by the verb in the main clause.*

18. b. *There is no subordinated clause possible after the end of the prompt. The word* aunque, *which sometimes requires the subjunctive, only governs* no le gustó; *the clause* la situación no tenía remedio *contains no expression or verb that would require the subjunctive to be used subsequently. The use of* que *after* tener *is one that is not translatable into English; more importantly, this use of* que *does not introduce subordinated clauses: it requires an infinitive.*

19. a. *In the clause introducing the subordinated noun clause, the verb* dijo *is used as a command, requiring the use of the subjunctive in the subordinated clause. Note that while* gustó *is an expression of emotion, it does not introduce the subordinated clause.*

20. c. *Whether one views the expression* es urgente *as either an impersonal expression of a command or an emotion, the subjunctive is required in the subordinated noun clause it introduces. The time frame requires the present subjunctive. None of the other options are in the subjunctive mood.*

7.16
1. d
2. e
3. g
4. a
5. b
6. h
7. c
8. j
9. f
10. i

7.17
1. d. *The subordinated adjective clause is introduced by a main clause whose verb is in the past and the antecedent* cuartos *is not specific, as it would be if it named particular room numbers.*

2. b. *The main clause, whose verb is in the present and is a verb of forbidding (as in a command or requirement, per the WEIRDO acronym), introduces a subordinated noun clause in which the present subjunctive must be used.*

3. b and c. *The subjunctive must be used because the verb in the main clause is one of emotion and, being in the past, requires the subjunctive in one of the past tenses of the subjunctive. Which is more correct depends on the way the time frame the speaker is recollecting, as can happen in English: either the service "had been slow" or it "was slow."*

4. c. *The verb in the main clause, in the imperfect indicative, is a verb of suspicion and thus only the imperfect subjunctive must be used in the subordinated noun clause.*

5. b. *The verb in the main clause is one of belief and is in the present. Therefore, the indicative must be used in the subordinated noun clause and must refer to the future.*

6. d. *The subordinated adjective clause modifies a non-specific antecedent—cuarto—; therefore, the subjunctive must be used. The main verb is in the present, and therefore the present subjunctive is the only option.*

7. b. *The adverbial expression* antes de que *always requires the subjunctive and the main verb is in the past, so the only option is the imperfect subjunctive.*

8. c. *The adverbial expression* para que *always requires the subjunctive. In this sentence, the main clause refers to the future, so the only subjunctive option admissible is the present subjunctive.*

9. a. *The expression* después de que *requires the subjunctive when the action of the verb that follows it is or was anticipated. In this sentence, the main clause is in the periphrastic future (i.e.,* ir + a + infinitive*) and therefore the action is anticipated in the future, requiring the present subjunctive.*

10. d. *The conditional in this hypothetical or contrary-to-fact sentence is presented first, to express the consequence of the if clause, whose verb must be in the imperfect subjunctive. Note that in this sentence, the two uses of the verb* haber *are not as helping verbs, but as existential verbs.*

11. b. *The adverbial expression* en caso de que *always requires the subjunctive to be used in the verb that it governs—in this case, two verbs:* querer *and* necesitar. *The main verb is in the present, so the only admissible option is the present subjunctive of both verbs. Note that the subjunctive is used for the verb* lavar, *in the next subordinated noun clause, because it is governed by the verbs* querer *and* necesitar.

12. c. *The adverb* cuando *requires the subjunctive when the verb following it expresses an action that is or was anticipated. In this sentence, the reference is to the future and thus only the present subjunctive is admissible.*

13. b. *The main clause expresses an emotion about a past event and thus the action following the adverb* aunque *expresses a mere report and therefore must be in the indicative and in the past tense.*

14. a. *The adverbial expression* para que *always requires the subjunctive in the verb that follows it. In this sentence, since the main verb –* hicimos *– is in the past, the imperfect subjunctive must be used.*

15. c. *The subordinated adjective clause modifies an antecedent that is suspected to be non-existent due to the use of* tendrá—*an example of a way of expressing probability in the present. However, it is not the probability aspect that requires the subjunctive, but rather the fact that there is an adjective clause modifying* cuarto, *the vague and likely non-existent antecedent.*

16. d. *The verb of recommendation, in the present, requires the present subjunctive to be used in the following subordinated noun clause.*

17. b. *The adjective clause modifies* los que *("those who") and is non-specific. That said, if the speaker knew of specific people in the group being addressed, because they had expressed an interest in fishing, then option (c) would be correct instead.*

18. b. *The adverb* cuando *requires the subjunctive when the verb following it expresses an action that is or was anticipated. In this sentence, the action of being ready is set future to the time the sentence is spoken and therefore only the present subjunctive is admissible.*

19. d. *The verb in the main clause is one of not allowing and is in the past. Therefore, the verb in the subordinated noun clause must be in the imperfect subjunctive.*

20. a. *The impersonal expression of necessity in the main clause is in the past and therefore the imperfect subjunctive is required in the subordinated noun clause.*

7.18
1. almorzábamos
2. cerraran
3. fuéramos
4. tuviera
5. buscaba
6. pudiéramos/pudiera
7. fuera
8. quedara
9. ayudara
10. llegáramos
11. escribiera
12. necesitaba
13. pudiéramos
14. había encontrado
15. sé
16. hubiéramos regresado
17. pudiera
18. empezara
19. digo
20. quita
21. sea
22. había gustado
23. pida

7.19
1. rinda
2. valía
3. exceda
4. fuera
5. tuvieras
6. enseñe
7. perdieran
8. subiera
9. hubiera
10. venda
11. quiebre

12. sea
13. compró
14. pagara
15. saldes
16. incluya
17. pudiera
18. esté
19. haya
20. hubiera

7.20
1. sufras
2. dejes
3. puedan
4. hubiera
5. acelere
6. sacara
7. vamos
8. surten
9. tenga
10. comiera
11. dejara
12. alimente
13. levante
14. diera
15. vieran
16. haya
17. dijera
18. firmen
19. tome
20. sigan

7.21
1. aprendiera
2. sabía
3. invitó
4. sabía

5. iba

6. rompiera

7. equivocara

8. quemara

9. explotara

10. indicó

11. prendiera

12. hiciera

13. saliera

14. tenía

15. enseñó

16. perdiera

17. estuviera

18. aparecieran

19. he aprendido

20. quisiera

21. fuera

22. hubieran inventado

23. obliguen

7.22
1. h
2. d
3. g
4. e
5. c
6. i
7. b
8. f
9. a
10. j

7.23
1. había manejado
2. había tomado
3. llevaran
4. gustaba

5. decidí

6. tuviera

7. hubiera/tuviera

8. gozara

9. seguían

10. enseñaran

11. íbamos

12. estaba

13. hubiera aprendido

14. saqué

15. fuera

16. tuviera

17. hubiera marcado/tuviera

18. necesitara

19. di

20. comprara

21. fuera

22. molestara

23. revisara

24. hiciéramos

25. tenía

7.24

1. c. *The expression* como si *always requires the imperfect subjunctive or pluperfect subjunctive, depending on the time frame. The time frame in this sentence is established as present (or aoristic) by the verb* viven. *Note that* compran *is within a relative clause and is not governed by* como si.

2. b. *The adverbial expression* hasta que *requires the subjunctive when the action following it is or was anticipated. Since* vamos, *the conjugated verb in the main clause, is in the present, forming a periphrastic future (a + infinitive), the action following* hasta que *is anticipated.*

3. a. *The main clause consists of an impersonal expression of emotion, in the present tense, introducing a subordinated noun clause, therefore the present subjunctive is the only option.*

4. d. *The main clause consists of a verb of recommending, in the preterite, introducing a subordinated noun clause, therefore the only admissible option is to use the imperfect subjunctive.*

5. c. *The use of a command in the main clause establishes the time frame as being present and the expression* una vez que *introduces an action that is anticipated as "about to have been performed," therefore only the present perfect subjunctive is admissible.*

6. a. *The main clause consists of an impersonal expression of necessity, or requirement, in the present tense, and introduces a subordinated noun clause; therefore only the present subjunctive is admissible.*

7. c. *The adverbial expression* mientras que *is introduced by the periphrastic future and therefore the action following this expression is anticipated. Only the present subjunctive is admissible.*

8. d. *The main clause contains a verb of emotion in the present and introduces a subordinated noun clause in which, therefore, only the present subjunctive is admissible. Note that* vaya *is the present subjunctive of the verb* ir—*and in turn forms what constitutes a periphrastic future subjunctive since it is used with* a + *infinitive.*

9. d. *The expression* aunque *can sometimes require the subjunctive, sometimes the indicative. In this sentence, the past time frame is established by* ayer *and this means that the rest of the sentence is a mere report of past action, "a matter of record," so to speak, and therefore only the indicative, in the past, is admissible.*

10. b. *The main clause is in the present tense and introduces a subordinated adjective noun clause which defines the non-specific antecedent* fuentes *and therefore only the present subjunctive is admissible in the subordinated clause.*

11. c. *The main clause consists of an impersonal expression of emotion, in the past, introducing a subordinated noun clause; therefore only the imperfect subjunctive option is admissible. Note that if the impersonal expression in the main clause were* Es horroroso, *then option (a) would be correct instead.*

12. c. *The main clause consists of an expression of non-doubt which, from a purely pragmatic, grammatical perspective, amounts to an equivalent of an assertion of belief. This excludes the use of the subjunctive. Furthermore, since the tense of the main verb,* cabía, *is in the past (imperfect indicative), the only admissible option presented is also the one that is in the imperfect indicative.*

13. b. *The main clause consists of a verb of negation in the present, requiring that the verb in the subordinated noun clause be in the present subjunctive.*

14. a. *The main clause consists of an impersonal expression of certainty, in the present, which requires that the indicative be used in the subordinated noun clause. Since the main verb is in the present, only the present indicative option is admissible. Note that if the impersonal expression in the main clause were* Era cierto, *then option (d) would be correct.*

15. d. *The past time frame is established in the main clause not by* dijo un científico *but by* era importante, *an impersonal expression of necessity or requirement which introduces a subordinated noun clause. Therefore, the imperfect subjunctive is the only admissible option. If the time frame of the main clause were present, then option (c) would be correct instead.*

16. c. *The tense of the main clause, being in the imperfect indicative, refers to an action that was taking place in the past. The antecedent* granjas, *because it is modified by the definite article* las, *is not vague and, therefore, the verb in the subordinated adjective clause modifying* granjas *must be in the imperfect indicative. That said, it is conceivable that many native speakers, in the flow of rapid speech, might say option (b), but this would be a native error due to the frequent phenomenon of mental ellipsis, that is, thinking of* granjas *that in the past and present produce organic vegetables.*

17. b, c, and d. *The choice depends upon how one is looking at the data about Cuba's agricultural output. Option (b) refers to past circumstances. Option (c) completes a statement of certainty about the present and option (d) looks to the future. Option (a) is inadmissible because it is in the subjunctive and the impersonal expression is one of certainty.*

18. a. *The main clause consists of a statement regarding probability in the past, which requires the subjunctive in the subordinated noun clause, which also must be in the past (i.e., in the imperfect subjunctive) due to the rules about sequence of tense.*

19. b. *The subordinated adjective clause modifies* medios, *which is non-specific or vague. The main verb,* necesitan, *is in the present and therefore only the present subjunctive option is admissible in the subordinated clause.*

20. c. *It is important to first note that the present time frame is established by* se va a acabar, *and not by the clause in the past introducing the indirect statement (i.e.,* Alguien dijo que*). Once that is clear, it should be apparent that the adverbial expression* a menos que, *introduced by the periphrastic future, means that the action following this expression is anticipated and therefore can only be completed grammatically by the present subjunctive. Option (d) would be correct if, instead of* va a acabar, *it were* iba a acabar.

7.25
1. sea
2. comience
3. pueda
4. ocurra
5. destruyera
6. baje
7. nieve
8. es
9. llueve
10. alcance
11. tenemos
12. oyeron
13. caiga
14. resbalara
15. pusiera
16. oigan
17. lloviera
18. salieran
19. tocara
20. haya

7.26
1. The waitress served us the desserts before we had finished eating.
2. It is important for the team to clean up the biohazardous liquid spill.
3. They will leave after we have seen the movie.
4. She needed a car that did not use a lot of gasoline.
5. The pilot hopes to land before it rains.
6. Doctor, when she wakes up, call me, please.
7. She wants him to deposit the funds in her savings account.
8. We prefer a room that has a balcony with a beach view.
9. I told the nurse to bring my mother another pillow.
10. They let me exchange that wine for this one even though I did not have the receipt.

7.27
1. A menos que la cliente tenga un recibo, no podemos darle una devolución en efectivo.
2. Le molestaba que la pantalla se le siguiera congelando.
3. Su padre quería una camioneta que tuviera un reproductor de discos compactos.
4. Les pedí que me reemplazaran el teclado.
5. Mi mamá debería haber comido alimentos que tuvieran menos grasas y sodio.
6. Es increíble que algunos no crean a/duden de los científicos.
7. Los niños esperan que deje de llover pronto para que puedan salir a jugar.
8. Se alegraban los ingenieros de que se hubiera aceptado su diseño.
9. ¿Hay alguna aplicación que me permita transferir fondos de un banco a otro?
10. No hubo/había nadie en la tienda que supiera arreglar mi teléfono celular.